IN PROTEST
150 POEMS FOR HUMAN RIGHTS

Edited by Helle Abelvik-Lawson, Anthony Hett and Laila Sumpton

Published 2013 by the Human Rights Consortium, School of Advanced Study, University of London.
Senate House, Malet Street, London WC1E 7HU
www.sas.ac.uk/hrc/

ISBN 978-0-9575210-3-2

Contents

Acknowledgements

First and foremost, we would like to thank the hundreds of people who collectively submitted over 600 poems for us to read, review, and reflect on. We were by turns moved, awed and impressed.

Many thanks to the academic staff at the School of Advanced Study who have contributed to the selection process: Dr Damien Short, Dr Corinne Lennox, and Professor Warwick Gould. Their time is extremely precious and their insights were invaluable. The administrative staff at the Human Rights Consortium and Institute of Commonwealth Studies also worked tirelessly to manage the submissions and selection process. Without Chloë Pieters and Robert Kenyon, none of this would have been possible.

We are grateful to Jon Millington for the work he did in disseminating the call for poems to the Institute of English Studies' literary contacts and networks.

The School of Advanced Study's Publications team has nursed this publication along every step of the way: it simply would not have been possible without the dedication of Kerry Whitston, Emma Bohan, Valerie Hall, Emily Morrell, Zoe Holman and Maureen McTaggart.

Paul Sherreard at Spread the Word has offered this project huge amounts of support and time.

A special thanks to both Ruth Padel for her foreword and to Sigrid Rausing for her afterword. The anthology is perfectly introduced and concluded by their touching contributions.

We are extremely grateful to Susi Bascon who not only connected us to David Ravelo but also brought the anthology to Sigrid Rausing's attention.

Many thanks to Carol Ann Duffy for offering us the use of her poem 'The Woman in the Moon', a lyrical addition to the anthology. We would also like to thank Arc Publications for permitting us to reprint 'Frontiers', by Chrissie Gittins; to the *Asia Literary Review*, for permitting us to reprint 'No Further', by Chrissie Gittins; to Bloodaxe Books for permitting us to reprint Moniza Alvi's 'Hanging'; and to Random House for permitting us to reprint Ruth Padel's 'The Prayer Labyrinth'. The anthology is all the richer as a consequence.

Reprint credits

'Hanging', originally printed in Moniza Alvi, *Europa* (Bloodaxe, 2008), www.bloodaxebooks.com.

'The Woman in the Moon' by Carol Ann Duffy originally published in *Granta* 103, autumn 2008, and in *The Bees* (Picador, 2011). Reprinted with permission from the author.

'No Further' by Chrissie Gittins was originally published in *Armature* (Arc Publications, 2003).

'Frontiers' by Chrissie Gittins was originally published in the *Asia Literary Review*, no.21, autumn 2011, www.asialiteraryreview.com.

'The Prayer Labyrinth' taken from *The Mara Crossing* by Ruth Padel (Chatto & Windus, 2012). Reprinted by permission of Ruth Padel and The Random House Group Limited.

Foreword

Ruth Padel

'After great pain, a formal feeling comes,' wrote Emily Dickinson. One miracle of being human is the way our need for meaning is met by our equally powerful need for pattern. Each culture made sense of the stars by figures they saw in them: the Greeks saw myths, like Orion. Chinese astronomers saw four regions presided over by mythic animals: Azure Dragon, Black Tortoise, White Tiger and Vermilion Bird. We are pattern-making animals, driven to make sense of the world around us, however dark and painful, by finding order, form and rhythm in what we see and feel.

One name for that is poetry. Poetry combines two of the deepest human needs: to tell our pain, and to make sense of it. Deprived of everything else, we turn to the power to put words together, express what goes on, inside and outside, and make of it a pattern we can share.

A poem is language under pressure: the charged, memorable patterning of words in the smallest possible space. Made out of need and vulnerability, by burning away the peripherals, a poem calls attention to how we think about what is human. For those who, on behalf of us all, defend the rights of being human, a poem is one of the most resonant and basic human tools.

This anthology brings together voicings of experience which most of its readers will be lucky enough not to know, first-hand. Yet elements in them speak to all our lives. 'This is the hour of lead,' Emily Dickinson's poem about pain and form continues: 'remembered, if outlived, / As freezing persons recollect the snow: / first chill, then stupor / then the letting go.'

In the hour of lead, it seems, what comes to our aid is the overwhelming desire to join other people by sharing the music of what is happening to us, now. The poems are particular lettings go, specific to each terrible situation. But they are also universal. They are the human voice responding to the human condition.

Introduction

Who we are

In 2012, the Human Rights Consortium (HRC) at the School of Advanced Study, University of London and the Keats House Poets collaborated on several events that brought together human rights and poetry, including a successful Human Rights Poetry Slam at the Bloomsbury Festival – an annual celebration of London's literary, cultural and intellectual centre. The HRC and Keats House Poets realised that poetry could bring human rights issues to a whole new audience and vice versa. The Human Rights Poetry Project was therefore set up and this unique human rights poetry anthology was launched.

The Keats House Poets, established in 2010, are a London-based poetry collective consisting of eight poets who are supported by the Keats House Museum in Hampstead. Two of these poets, Anthony Hett and Laila Sumpton, have been working with HRC staff for over a year to develop the Human Rights Poetry Project. This anthology has also been supported by Spread the Word, London's writer's development agency, who have awarded prizes to four of the anthology's poets in aid of their professional development: Camila Fiori, Nick Makoha, Susan Wood and Xidu Heshang.

Despite being a departure from the typical work of the HRC – which engages in academic research on a variety of human rights issues, from environmental rights to refugee law – the Human Rights Poetry Project caught the attention of a number of human rights academics, NGO campaigners, and other professionals interested in the use of language and art in human rights activism. It also gave poets from all over the world the chance to write to the human rights theme, doubtless igniting for many an interest in the legal, social and cultural complexities of human rights as an academic discipline.

Why human rights poetry?

This anthology hopes to engage both poets and human rights academics and practitioners in exploring what their respective disciplines can offer each other.

The academic discipline of human rights is a broad multidisciplinary subject that covers everything from the right to clean water to the right to be free from 'torture or cruel, inhuman or degrading treatment'. It engages with law, politics, economics, philosophy, psychology, sociology and anthropology, among other established disciplines. A common understanding of the broader concept is that 'we have human rights simply because we are human'.

Behind the rationale for creating a human rights poetry anthology was the sense that poetry, and creative use of language more broadly, is a powerful way to 'move people from apathy to action'. Human rights lawyers, campaigners and advocates carefully select their words to do just this; telling the stories of individuals who have had their rights violated, or who are fighting discrimination in some form.

On the literary and creative side, the editors recognised that great literature also creates a sense of solidarity within the reader: the author reaches out of the page to say something important and relevant – even universal – about the human condition. This is where poetry and human rights are related: empathy and solidarity, unsurprisingly, are essential in human rights work.

The process

The 'call for poems' was released in February 2013, and over the next three months, poets from around the world offered submissions. The Keats House Poets, Institute of English Studies and HRC utilised their extensive academic, NGO and literary networks to reach hundreds of organisations and thousands of individuals. The result was over 600 submissions from over 18 different countries, including China, Chile, Australia, Canada, India and South Africa. Handwritten poems were received from those without an email address or access to a computer. One poem came from La Picota prison in Colombia. The poet, David Ravelo, a Colombian human rights defender, had received death threats before facing a trial described as irregular by lawyers and international human rights organisations; he has been sentenced to 18 years in prison. He wrote 'The firmament, La Picota Prison, 23rd January 2013' for human rights philanthropist Sigrid Rausing's birthday.

The editors spent a gruelling three weeks reading hundreds of anonymised submissions, reflecting on poetic merit and whether poems clearly portrayed a human rights theme. The variety of ways poets chose to interpret the broad theme of 'human rights' was of particular interest, and though poems have been organised into 13 thematic chapters, many poems easily cut across these themes.

Poems exercising subtlety were chosen – they allow the reader to explore the issue and reach their own decision. Additionally, poems showing respect for the groups and individuals represented, and poems appreciating the complexity of intertwined human rights themes and their cultural, political and economic contexts, were singled out particularly.

The anthology

The anthology speaks to the extensive array of human rights issues throughout history, from the trans-Atlantic slave trade up to the current war in Syria. Some in this collection unflinchingly tell of the horrors endured by victims and survivors of human rights abuses using personal testimony, such as Alireza Abiz's 'The kindly interrogator' and researched testimony as in Richard Scott's 'Cutting season'. In telling these stories and bearing witness to atrocities, poets open up dialogue and ask for action. The poems here show the cruelty of humanity, but also its resilience.

Reading this anthology, you will move across continents from Chile to Australia, from North Korea to Sierra Leone to the streets of London – constantly finding common themes in each poem's protest for global equality and freedom. You will hear a range of voices – the child questioning the news and what version of history to believe; the testimonies of victims and survivors; the reporter's voice both close yet detached; the human rights cynic; and the oppressor's justification. Some of the poems, such as 'Greenies' and 'Thank you for visiting Deathminster', express contemporary human rights concerns using the surprising technique of humour: these poems take on the voice of the oppressor and the powerful in order to undercut and ridicule their stance.

While the abuses of regimes and the State are well-charted in the poems, the stories of those who have lost their land and are homeless, detained or enslaved, throughout history and up to now are also presented.

Often poems express the honest and thoughtful voices of those who have not suffered human rights violations themselves, but feel very deeply when others have. Jaki McCarrick's 'The kestrel' takes readers to the morning when the news broke of Troy Davis's execution in the United States. The poem contemplates the inter-species killing as a metaphor for the inhumanity of the death sentence: 'that everything is prey, and that instinctively / each species will not protect itself'. Similarly, Alyson Hallett's poem 'To the men of Guantanamo Bay' describes feelings of safety and happiness and wanting to 'take this morning and fold it / into an envelope' for the inmates.

Highlights

There is not room in this introduction to praise every excellent poem, but this section shares some highlights, listed in the same order as the thematic sections.

Starting the collection is the 'Expression' section, which contains poems that discuss the way that human rights are portrayed through stories and images, and the 'long wrangling over definitions' of key concepts like genocide (offered to us by Kathy Zwick's poem 'Mirages of meaning'). Within this theme, Richard Tyrone Jones's cynically humorous poem 'We need a victim' describes the difficulty of choosing the right language and story to tell in a human rights campaign; 'because if they lose, we lose, right?' – reflections no doubt shared by many human rights activists and campaigners. 'Swollen' by Camila Fiori describes someone who wants to speak out against what is happening around her; imagery and simile are used to great effect: 'Instead, she would swallow / collect them inside her / Like swords hung on a wall'.

Poems in the 'History' chapter reflect on atrocities and rights violations past, but not forgotten, from a contemporary perspective. Joe Massingham's poem shows poignantly how 'the right to bear arms' has transformed from its inception 'Under the Constitution', connecting readers in the last stanza to modern-day Newtown in Connecticut where it has become 'the right to kill the innocent / and shoot their carers and protectors'.

Key themes in the research of academics working within the HRC emerged in the 'Land' chapter, where poets explored environmentalism, climate change, mining and indigenous rights in Commonwealth countries and the Occupied Palestinian Territories (OPT). The editors are grateful to be able to reprint in this chapter Carol Ann Duffy's haunting and devastating poem 'The woman in the moon', first published by Granta in 2008.

'Snake guarding a watering hole' by Susan Wood very visually and concisely introduces the reader to Aboriginal artist Turkey Tolson, living in a resettlement area beyond his ancestors' traditional country, 'to which he has no claim / other than this painting'. The link here between land and traditional culture is made all the more clear through its tragic severance.

'Acts respecting Indians' by Shane Rhodes is a 'found poem', using words from the Government of Canada's Indian Act and so exposing the indigenous dispossession and absurdities enshrined in settler-conceived law: 'providing no Indian shall be / deemed lawfully in possession / of any "Indian lands" / providing all such Indians / shall henceforward cease / to be Indians.'

In quite a different geographical context, natural imagery is melodically engaged in Barbara Cumbers' 'Thirst fugue', written in the style of Paul Celan's 'Death fugue', with equally haunting refrains of 'your mulberry tree Khadija / your clear pools Ibrahim' throughout the poem, denoting struggles over scarce water resources within the OPT.

In a clear sign of the times, many poets submitted on the theme of 'Exile', and this chapter explores migration, its criminalisation, and the precarious sense of belonging felt by those seeking asylum or migrating for a better life. Poems that stood out particularly included Ruth Padel's 'The prayer labyrinth' which was based on research into the UK's asylum system. She blends mythology and testimony to tell appalling stories of seeking asylum: 'they say you don't belong. They give you / a broken finger, a punctured lung'.

Keith Jarrett, winner of the Human Rights Poetry Slam at the 2012 Bloomsbury Festival, submitted 'Asylum cocktails' – a poem that masterfully takes the prejudiced language of those who define asylum law, and uses it to undermine their position, showing us a 'double-standards dance'. It tackles the complexities of both exile and sexuality: 'they say fear is about / ticking boxes & not boys loving boys', and uses a clever form where line-end words make up the quotation that inspired it.

Many submissions on the theme of 'War' were received, with a large number on Syria alone, indicating the resonance this conflict, ongoing at the time of writing, has for many. James Byrne's 'Fragments for Ali' stood out for its crafted lyricism and ability to transport the reader beyond the news to where civilians struggle to live and ask 'how do new buds grow from beheaded flowers?'. 'Srebrenitsa and Ratko Mladich' is also a hard-hitting poem which uses bleak imagery to tell its tale, ending with the hope of redress for the victims of the Balkan wars: 'and now a murderer is exposed for the world to see'.

Many poets clearly felt very affected by children's human rights issues. Pat Borthwick's 'Patio' uses onomatopoeia to great effect: 'That chip chip chip, tink, tink, tap' is the soundtrack to a young Indian boy's life, labouring in quarries for paving stones destined for '*Liverpool / Hull, London*'; not just places he will never know, but 'Words / Naresh will never understand' – a small hint of inevitable life-long illiteracy. A shocking poem about poverty, David Lee Morgan's 'Dead babies' is a visceral piece of second-person storytelling and a compelling call to action that would lend itself to performance. Its ending has echoes of television campaigns that seek to elicit a real-time comprehension of the statistics: 'This poem is fourteen dead babies long'.

The 'Sentenced' chapter pulls together poems about both life and death sentences from around the world. Beyond 'The firmament' and 'The kestrel', another highlight is Moniza Alvi's poem 'Hanging', which lyrically observes the elusiveness of justice and the brutality of the death penalty, and how much is in the balance: 'the world is hanging'; 'the countries adhere to the globe – just'; 'the ink clung in the nib'.

The theme of 'Slavery' was immediately apparent: one of the great tragedies of the current state of human rights is that slavery, although legally outlawed in all countries, has not been abolished in practice and exists in many forms, including bonded labour and sex trafficking. The latter is explored in 'Vegetable' by Kayleigh Kavanagh through the metaphor of factory farming: a victim of the international sex trade is the eponymous vegetable that is 'pulled from the bed', 'thrown back into the pile' with 'false hormones pumped in'.

Many submissions explored women's rights issues. Hollie McNish, runner-up in the closely fought Slam of 2012, sent us her poem 'Embarrassed', an engaging personal testimony about breastfeeding – the advantages of which are mentioned in Article 24 of the Convention of the Rights of the Child. In 'this country of billboards hoarded with "tits"', where women's bodies are over-sexualised and commoditized, she is embarrassed to breastfeed her baby in public 'in case that small flash of flesh might offend'. The well-paced performance poem notes the scandal of companies selling powdered milk 'in countries where water runs dripping in filth'; the poem finally contemplating why on earth 'we're now paying for the one thing that's always been free'.

Shamshad Khan's 'Angel on the right' helps us understand the messages of peace and respect for women in Islam, sentiments which are often at odds with many cultural interpretations. She ends with the hope that 'the angel on her husband's left shoulder / will have nothing to record tonight'.

In the 'Regimes' chapter, Nick Makoha's 'A crocodile eats the sun' is a firm favourite; a harrowing poem about Uganda with powerful imagery. The beauty of the writing is juxtaposed against the subject matter, and despite the difficult theme it is a joy to read and re-read. The final line 'our bodies still rest in your jaws' leaves the reader with a strong image and an uneasy feeling.

Economic rights are well represented in the 'Workers' chapter. The somewhat esoteric 'Plum rain' by Paul Adrian is a fascinating reminder of the impact of the supply chain, linking farming and fashion cycles, from workers wishing for rains for a good 'cotton season', to 'fingers worrying' over 'next season's colours'. Liang Yujing's ode 'To money' is clever and humorous, beginning the journey with anthropomorphic wordplay – 'in America you're a herd / of wild bucks galloping from Wall Street to banks to companies' – but ending with 'forty thousand of broken fingers / are scattered along the Pearl River, fingers of the workers'.

In the 'Inequality' chapter, issues such as homelessness, hunger and lesbian, gay, bisexual, transgender and intersex (LGBTI) rights are expertly explored. Benjamin Hayes's 'Marriage equality', a skilfully written haiku poem, puts it succinctly: 'Equal marriage rights. / Two people love each other. / None of your business.'

To the editors one of the most exciting themes was the final one, 'Protest'. In Douglas Dunn's 'The demonstration' the right of free speech and freedom of assembly is challenged: 'the police squared up to the students / Who waved their banners and bottles of mineral water'. In a brilliant and surreal twist the protesters emerge victorious: 'then the policemen lay down and the students carried them away'. Particularly pertinent for this anthology is the message of Caroline's Rooney's poem 'Al Hurriya fi Masr', which describes the coming together of poets 'to compose the coming of revolution'; and calls for the people 'to become a living human poem.' Another powerful poem in this final section is Andrew Walton's 'Grândola Vila Morena, 2013'. The title takes the name of the banned song played on the radio that started the bloodless 'Carnation' revolution against the authoritarian regime in Portugal on 25 April 1974, so called because the people followed the song's signal to come out into the streets and put carnations in the barrels of soldiers' guns. The title suggests a more contemporary resonance and the final stanza, where 'We, the masses, are rising once more / In the spirit of nineteen-seventy four', shows that the people still can 'shudder the seats of power'.

Throughout the collection's 13 chapters the urgency and agony of human rights violations – both for victims and witnesses and those that *feel* and empathise with them – is palpably clear. What truly surges through the volume is a great sense of solidarity with other human beings.

The future

Many of these poems mention towns or names that might be unfamiliar, but will lead you to uncover human rights violations old and new. When putting together this anthology the editors wanted to inspire poetry activism – poetry that teaches readers about human rights abuses, and moves people from apathy to action. We want this anthology to be shared with colleagues, students, friends or family to inspire action for change. There are incredible individuals and organisations actively campaigning on all of the themes represented in this book, and we would love these poems to be used to explain the human issues at the centre of what they do.

We feel that each poem truly has the power to become a 'living human poem' and would wish them to become living campaigners for each of their issues. Maybe they will call you to march with them, to share their unique stories, to find out more, or to get involved in making change.

These poems will not lie sleeping on your shelf; they cry out to be shared and they want to inspire.

The Editors
Helle Abelvik-Lawson
Anthony Hett
Laila Sumpton

Expression

The orphan as adult

PD Lyons

my eyes were not green for you
I did not rebel or lead
never even learned to read.
children dropped from me
in a pain no one cared about.
my years marked by long days and short lives.

as if expecting greeting, you return.
as if your photographs meant something
other than a young girl momentarily annoyed
her world same now as it was then
a place where things just are the way they are.

my eyes were not green for you
only an accident of birth
same as your own.

For Afghanistan

Running order: BBC Radio 4 News at 8am, 1 August 2012

Mantz Yorke

Eight female badminton players are charged with not trying
to win their matches, or trying to fix results so they face
preferred opponents in the semi-final. Against the spirit
of the Olympics, netting the shuttle and hitting it out of court
had prompted the crowd to boo, whistle and bellow 'Off!'.

Michael Phelps has, for some, become 'the greatest Olympian',
with nineteen medals, fifteen of them gold. And Team GB's
failure so far to gain one gold may later be redeemed
by the women's pair on Dorney Lake, or Bradley Wiggins
repeating his triumphant time-trialling in the Tour de France.

Gore Vidal, the novelist, script-writer and acid wit, has died
in Los Angeles, aged 86. A clip is played of him protesting
at the lack of protest against 'The United States of Amnesia'
suspending constitutional freedoms of speech and assembly,
and implicitly imposing a religion as a condition for success.

Amnesty International claims that the Syrian government's
forces have abused human rights in Aleppo, with tanks,
artillery, helicopter gunships and fighter aircraft opening fire
on peaceful protesters and bystanders, including children.
And now, it's reported, a large military column is heading in.

Down from third spot on the bulletin at six, Save the Children
and World Vision estimate that in the Sahel the high price
of food may lead some eighteen million inhabitants to starve.

The tocsins, here muffled by gold, have no resonance
for those who will struggle on, oblivious, and may not win.

Naming

Seni Seneviratne

I want to hear their names. The names
of the ones who were sleeping. The names
of the ones who are wrapped in blankets.

Not his name. Not the soldier
with his 9mm pistol and his M4 rifle
outfitted with a grenade launcher.

Not the name of his wife who reaffirmed
her love after the fatal dawn, nor the names
of his children nor their schoolmates.

Not the name of the 'buddy' who had lost a leg
a few days before, nor the neighbour who said,
'That kid's got the biggest heart anywhere.'

Not the name of the defence lawyer
who believes there will be insufficient evidence
because the victims' fingerprints were burned.

Nazia, Mohamed, Khudaydad, Nazar, Payendo,
Robeena, Nabia, Shatarina, Zahra, Essa, Masooma,
Farida, Palwasha, Esmatullah, Faizullah, Akhtar.

Your names. Because you were sleeping and now
you are wrapped in blankets. Because everything
has changed and everything will stay the same.

Banned UK search terms

Ken Evans

> *(China's Vice-President Xi Jinping's absence from public life makes Chinese internet providers censor word searches based on his name and 'Back ache' to avert conspiracy theories.)*

Vatican peephole

Bikiniless Royals

Olympics pointless

True jobless totals

University shutdown

Unaffordable housing

Child starves, Mytholmroyd.

Horseburger makers

Drone death video

'Dignitas' vouchers

Zero sport legacy

Pussy Riot copycats

Funeral bloodlust

Dirty Bomb phone app

Hillsborough anarchists

Chain jobless to badgers –

Word search tazerers

Word tsar delete chiefs

Search term jihadis

Conspiracy fairies.

Speech found

Sue Guiney

Wooden parliamentary walls bring privileges.
White papers, blue screens do not.

Criticism. Questioning. Agreeing to disagree.
Civilized concepts we teach our children
then punish them for voicing once they're old.

There is no thought without speech.
There is no progress without thought.

While some fight for their right to read and write,
others boast of rights they only think they have.

Those cages barring birdsong can be invisible, too.

Quotidian

Usha Raman

Terrorism is a way of life
like my morning toast
healthy whole wheat
masking the grinding of bones
salted with the perspiration
from the brows and arms and legs
of suicide prone farmers;
or the orange juice
imported from reconstituted republics
into colonies of consumption
their choreographed dreams exploited
by real estate developers
selling bits and gigs and terabytes
of mindspace.
Our everydays, our lives,
our lifestyles
cannot do without the products
of habitual violence.
It spices my rudeness
as I disregard
the helplessly signaling pedestrian
in my workday haste.
It seasons my impatience
as I wave away the reaching arm
of the little beggar girl
at the traffic junction.
It garnishes the arguments
that heat tabletops
at business lunches, discussions
of Others who have
Not quite made the cut.
It spikes the ratings graphs
of television shows
that hold us hostage,
primed as we are
for their distant drama.

Turning a blind eye

Alia' Afif Kawalit

I try to make myself at home after seeing your heartfelt smile
I sit and you offer me a mango imported from Bombay.
First you plough it with a knife,
then with a spoon you carve the flesh.
A spoonful to muffle
a never-dormant vent with familiar sweetness.
I swallow my barren words like bubbles that bloat in my throat.
You try to make sense of my case. Stranger. Your voice still
awaits similarities. Maybe there aren't any.
I avert my eyes to the TV set and mention how good it is
to have Indian channels. *You feel at home.*
Compassionately, you look for an Arabic programme.
and flip through the channels with an excited smile.
You stop on an image. I press my lips.
Fuming on Aljazeera. A body is burnt from head to toe.
I avert my eyes towards the torn mango skin.
What else, I ask.
What else, you say.

Mirages of meaning

Kathy Zwick

Can a dictionary decide
when and what is *'genocide'*
or, just bookmark for another later date?
Undulating desert sands and brazen skies
distort the moral hour glass,
scratchy sand in Darfur's clockworks,
long wrangling over definitions.

Wafting, rippling visions of deferred responsibility
bookmarked for another later date,
somewhere between *'gelatine'* and *'gesticulate'* –
wafting, nebulous mirages of meaning.
Shifting dunes, neglect migrating with the winds.
Creeping, encroaching.
What has this ancient lake bed seen?

Ten years on. Humanity on hold.

Kashmir

Usha Raman

The edges of the textbook map
bleed quietly into my studious mind
like ink on blotting paper,
while scribes scratch out
the noisy newsprint
that a hurrying-away boy tosses onto my balcony
every morning.
Social studies lessons
taught without emotion
full of numbing dates and
unpronounceable names
blind our children
to the devouring reasons of state.
Young men in the northern hills
imagining insurgency;
desperately demonstrating mothers
echoing those from other, no-less-dirty, wars,
trying to reclaim
the lost youth of their generations;
and the elders left to mourn
behind veils and worn-out blankets,
their stories eclipsed
by the questions and answers
in civil services examinations
that push all of life
into a dull green paper folder
to be filed away
in the twisting corridors
of power,
where they lie, forgotten
until they make their way into
reports, leached of flesh and blood
turned into simple, stark,
monochromatic typescript.

Parsing

Richard Tyrone Jones

They took away her audience; she composed just for herself
They took away her laptop; she reverted to the pen
They took away her paper; she wrote on her arm
They took away her knife; she framed lines inside her head

They took away her time; she turned the rhythm of her labour
to the chant of her existence. They cut out her tongue.
She composed in her head; they lobotomised.
Still her aphasic dreams, of birds and better men, rhymed.

They took away her breath. Her blood schooled the soil;
its saplings stretched their wings through her
to scribble on the sky.

Swollen

Camila Fiori

There was a woman, collected words:
long words, short words, hard-edged
words that, spoken, would score
deep grooves in her palate.

Instead she would swallow;
hoard them inside her. Like swords
hung on a wall, echoes
in a grotto they bore history.

Quietly roaring they sucked
mute lines in her cheeks,
written from under – borderland
thinning, skin slug-sallow.

Plump words, shunting organs
flat to the frame that contained her,
knocking her off the delicate line
she drew around all of their secrets.

Her throat – she maintained,
unscathed by the lip of a word,
cruel consonant – stayed soft
Eternal vowels

puckered in silent pockets
hung from the hollows
sunk in her skull – windows
dunned, where light once flickered.

Eyes, slit to a smile;
a shallow hum
between her lips,

                    a gap

We need a victim

Richard Tyrone Jones

We've got to choose our battles carefully –
because if we lose, it's the victims who lose.
So this report on child abuse:
We need a victim to talk to –
an actual victim,
but not just any old victim.
You've got to choose your warriors carefully,
because if they lose, we lose, right?

We need a victim with perfect recall –
names, dates, etc. Autistic, preferably,
but not too autistic. Ideally one who kept a diary.
We need an Anne Frank of child abuse.

We need a victim who'll stand up to cross-questioning.
Someone so strong that the systematic
sexual and psychological abuse didn't crush them –
else it's the rest of the media who'll eat them alive.
of course they must still cry on demand.

After all we have to been seen to act sensitively on this

We need a victim who isn't open to accusations
of being after the cash – someone originally
from an orphanage, but who later came into
some unknown Dickensian uncle's inheritance.

We need a victim – one good-looking,
to grab the red-tops' headlines,
but not so good-looking you yourself
almost sympathise with the paedos.

We need a victim. The old one's damaged goods.
We need the perfect victim.
Luckily, there are so many
we shouldn't have any difficulty
convincing one to come forward.

Just don't put too much pressure on them.
Softly-softly now. We don't want to scare them off.

/ Or else the rest of the media will just eat them alive. Anything else, and
they're just not victim enough.

In the tradition of *The Star*

Linda Cosgriff

This poem is censored.
I cannot mention _____ _____,
a banned person; _____ _____
or _____ _____.
Their organisation, ____ ____,
may not be discussed under
the current State of Emergency.
I cannot include a photo,
share details, describe actions.

I give you blank space:

in protest.

History

Abandoned property

Sohaib Mirza

They were books
Irrelevant to some
Relevant to others
It was a little known event
An historical event
They were collected
From people's home
Books of great significance
The books contained
Details, descriptions, pictures
Of events long ago
By removing the books
Was in effect
Removing their history
Removing their roots
Books marked with 'AP'
Abandoned property
When they were not

1959

Mary Anne Perkins

> *It was not until October 2012 that three Kenyan survivors of the Hola massacre of March 1959 won the right to take legal action against the British government for the torture inflicted by wardens and officials of the detention camp.*

Rising eleven, we've got the hang of things.
Heads, it's the grammar school; tails, it's not.
We've sworn allegiance to God and the Queen
– you with your toggle, I with my Girl Guide tie
ironed flat at the knot.

Watching TV, we learn our enemies –
most of them red and not much to choose between
except that the Indians shoot at wagon
trains and Ruskies fire puppies into space.
The Americans win in any case,

but everyone knows the Brits are best.
Everything's different here. We're kind
to animals and won the war by playing fair.
Besides, the Mother of Parliaments
lives somewhere near.

Now Grandpa says there's trouble in Africa:
somebody beat the Kenyan blacks too hard
and now they're dead. He doesn't believe
they died of pneumonia – nobody heard of *that*
making holes in your head.

Who knows?
– says Dad, who's washing the car again –
They were probably rogues.

Guests of Africa

Philip Bateman

Why do you ask, my son, of matters which should not pass our lips
and to which no answer comes?
Why, my child, do you speak of coloureds, of servants who call you 'Boss'
     when they are old and grey and wise, and you a fledgling, a seedling,
nurtured from the same earth bed?

Your tousled brows are furrowed like mielie fields in Spring
but filled with shadows murmuring wars of dark and light
yet your glow is of an African summer that speaks of bursting Mopani fruit,
of spreading baobabs and secrets infinite.

Today you offer tousled thoughts, burning and tearing, a lion's pacing,
a hunger that will not be stilled.
Do not gaze at me, my son, for it smoulders the soul and stirs up
veld fires beyond all thinking.

We did not create the streams, the silver African mist, the throb of singing
     drums.
We did not build the huts of mud, nor spawn the herds that drift across the
     sky.

We are the wanderers of newer times, voyagers from another world,
guests of ancient Africa.

Finding Australia

Cath Drake
(for Miss Brockman)

We learned the directions of the compass, names of brave sailors
who sounded like philosophers, coloured in their sailing ships,
drew map after map that tracked noblemen spun by wild winds
who tried to find spices, and almost found Australia.

Unwieldy ships were washed up on far flung reefs or islands.
When finally they found it, they put up flags on hilltops, nailed
plaques to trees. Captain Stirling was certain he'd found Perth,
so certain he brought boatloads of people down the Swan River

to witness it, commission paintings, build houses, forge roads.
Australia was young and proud, our future was on a plate.
We filled our project books with drawings of early settlers
in smart soldier outfits, women in long skirts and bonnets.

They kept on finding as they trekked through rugged terrain
to discover more and more of what had not yet been found.
We coloured in more maps, listened to stories of hardship
when tattered men perished for us in search of an inland sea.

Then our eccentric year nine social studies teacher whispered:
Terra nullus? terra nullus? Australia was not discovered:
there were already people here right across the beaches,
plains, forests and deserts, who knew every bump and echo.

She showed us slides of black men in chain gangs, eyes disjointed
with shock, frightened black women in shift dresses, archives
of river poisonings and battles for land where only one side won.
She showed us modern photos of black people on reserves

with scattered rubbish and makeshift houses staring out of the dust,
told of a whole generation of children taken from their parents.
There weren't any pictures of brave men in sailing ships.
I wondered if we'd dreamt it all and what else they lied about.

Under the cross

Marina Sanchez

Franco's mighty stone cross rises
from a summit in the sierra,
his war memorial
a remainder, surveying
the landlocked capital below.

The Generalissimo's portrait hung
next to the Pope's in every classroom.
We prayed for both before and after
every lesson, every hour,
every day and in daily mass.

The nun who taught History
would show us her skin
scored by burns and cuts,
spitting her blame, '*Los Rojos*',
the Republicans, dad's side.

I see him still on the red earth,
among the olive groves,
looking at his distant birthplace,
unable to visit surviving relatives,
worried he could be arrested.

In exile, his heart faltered
but the red, yellow and mauve
still flies: in rallies, in concerts
and in some public buildings,
his *tricolor* flies, the *tricolor* flies.

Guernica

Jaki McCarrick

> *'Guernica!' was the headline of a Barcelona newspaper published the day after the*
> *Madrid bombings of 11 March 2004. I was in Barcelona the night before the dead were*
> *to be buried, amid vociferous anti-war protests.*

In a Catalonian spring that has no warmth
marchers are drumming to remind the sleeping
that handfuls of sand will rattle the morning.

Candles illumine a government building,
drawings, red roses anoint a circle,
bloodied sheets line municipal squares.

A newspaper editor remembers a horse
yawning in a painting of a Basque town
while a vigil-keeper weeps through the shawl of her hands.

Silent courage

Lorraine Caputo

The Saturday market streets are full of the
bargaining for housewares & chickens
in the sh-shs & clicks of Ixil

I wind past the crowded stalls to the church
Stone dust drifts through the nave
from a scaffold in the apse
It glitters in the filtered sunlight

On the left wall, Christ slumps upon a large crucifix
Small even-armed wooden crosses surround him,
names engraved of those victims
of the government abuses here
the disappeared, the kidnapped
the tortured, the assassinated

I sit on a nearby bench
studying their lives
Seventeen years of documentation
from 1974 to 91
many from 80, 81, 82

The clang of hammer upon rock
reverberates through this sanctuary

I mentally count the crosses, row upon row
like a halo around the Savior
Now & again I look furtively over to those workers
One, two, three hundred
four hundred   & seventy   four
crosses   474 lives   474
victims   martyrs
474 deaths

EOKA Museum

John Daniel

Perhaps they were wrong,
the freedom fighters of Cyprus,
the hundred photos each in its small box
with flickering candles,
interrogated by the British, row after row,
the new museum with its white floors and grey models,
guerrillas crouching in caves.

Perhaps they were wrong,
the 22 year old Patatsos, Zakos and Michael
hanged together,
the 18 year old Pallikarides
hanged by the British.
fighting for union with Greece and for God.

Our hotel manager says the people don't like the priests.
They tell them to shave off their beards.
They want to be free of Athens and Ankara.
Perhaps the tall statue of Archbishop Makarios
will have to come down. Perhaps the museum
is wrong for the Turks coming through the green line
in long skirts like gypsies.

The British have gone.
They sit only in cafes, red-faced over their beers
but I think it is right to remember the torturers
as well as the heroes, to look at the rope
in its metal sheath hanging over the beam,
to re-enter the noose,
to know who I am.

Civilian executions, Minsk 1941

Eamonn Lynskey

Because your back is turned
your face will never be remembered,
woman with your wrists tied up,
the elbows of your cardigan
unravelling.

Because your face is shown
you will forever be remembered,
officer who reaches up,
adjusts the noose so that the drop
will take her weight.

Barely in the frame
a soldier hurries past the truck
intent on military duties,
doesn't bother to look up
before the shutter falls.

Roll call

Joan Michelson

'Consider whether this is a man.'
Primo Levi *Shema*

It's sixty-seven years since her parents
took her far from Europe. She was two,
young enough not to know her father,
then awaiting trial in Krakow, Poland.
Years later her sister, who was older,
traced her. Then she made the journey
to her past. In a newsprint photo, 1947,
she finds her father seated in a courtroom.
He's wearing heavy wartime headphones and looking
at a file of papers. She whispers, *Look up.*
Look at me. I'm your daughter. For half a year
he served as Kamp Kommandant of Auschwitz.
For mass murder, he was sentenced, hanged.
She can't let this rest, She gathers evidence
to prove him good. He eased some rules,
called off the killer dogs. Against the cold,
he allowed caps on during roll call.
One survivor named him *half an angel.*
She weeps. Her father followed orders from Himmler.

No further

Chrissie Gittins

While I stand naked in the bamboo hut
I am my father. Our freckles fuse,
our noses redden, our hair bleaches to sand.

He is marching in the Arakan, his friends
fall at his feet, they die quietly –
Jamchapel (Honeychurch), Windy (Breeze), Oscar (Wild).

At seventy-four my father fights battles in his pyjamas.
He wakes on the floor of his room.
A Lancaster bomber painted on a china plate

climbs the frail wall.
He is marching, the sweat stands on his brow,
his nose glistens. His squadron seeps across

a tea-plantation, one man is invited in to bathe.
My father sits naked in a tin bath.
I ladle water over my shoulders,

come to welcome the knife of water down my back.
The scrubbing brush will not rid my feet of grime,
it lines my toenails like kohl.

Should I wash my hair first or my bucket of clothes?
The tin of water is mine, to dowse my sandals,
to dribble down my legs, to scald away the heat.

Outside, a soldier rests a gun
across his narrow shoulders.
He will patrol the camp tonight.

After nine I will go no further than my hut
with its woven walls and roof of folded leaves.

Under the Constitution

Joe Massingham

The right to bear arms in Boston
is a right to resist the tyrant,
to defend oneself against the trespasser,
to demonstrate the self-evidence of freedom's truths.

The right to bear arms in Memphis
is a right to subjugate, oppress,
to assert oneself as racially superior,
to demonstrate the falsity of equality's truths.

The right to bear arms in Newport
is a claim of ancient lineage,
a statement of privilege and caste,
to demonstrate that 'equal' is an unequal term.

The right to bear arms in Harlem
is an invitation to the leveler, Death,
to share a fix with an unequal other
and demonstrate that only too late are we free.

The right to bear arms in Newtown
is a right to kill the innocent
and shoot their carers and protectors
before escaping by shooting oneself.

Land

Acts respecting Indians[1]

Shane Rhodes

In the interests of the Indians,
of wild grass
and dead or fallen timber,
the expression 'person'
means any individual
other than an Indian;
and the expression 'Indian'
means any male person
of Indian blood,
any child of such person,
any woman married to such person,
if they are Indians within
the meaning of this Act;
providing any Indian woman
marrying any other than an Indian
shall cease to be an Indian;
providing the property
of an unmarried Indian woman
shall descend as if she had been male;
providing for the arrest
and conveyance to school
of truant children;
providing they are not persons
to induce, incite or stir up
any three or more Indians;
providing they are not destitute
of the knowledge of God
or a future state of awards
and punishments;
providing they are not half-breeds
in Manitoba;
providing no Indian shall be
deemed lawfully in possession
of any 'Indian lands';
providing all such Indians
shall thenceforward cease
to be Indians.

---

1   All words are taken from the Government of Canada's Indian Act (An Act Respecting Indians)
    and its many amendments.

Snake guarding a water-hole

Susan Wood

Turkey Tolson an aboriginal
settled by the government at Papunya
where his tribe had never camped or hunted
painted this snake.
Its sides follow the desert's curve
for miles and miles of walkabout.
The dunes hunch and flow
to become snake
then are land again.
Only Turkey Tolson knows
where the desert ends
and the slow coils of unawakened
dream-time shift on
across a landscape
to which he has no claim
other than this painting.

Elegiac

Susan Wood

Charlie Tjapangati, Clifford Possum Tjapaltjarri
Tim Woods Tjampitjimpa...
the names half-stick to your tongue
familiar, domesticated like old dogs
uncles and men in dungarees
greasy to the elbow
or smelling of wood-dust
but just as you've got it
the name veers off into jarring corrugations
unseated
you spell it out like a child
wanting what you already know
the sly wolf dressed in grandma's clothes
the tubby bear climbing for honey
crooning his easy songs.

But in the end
Charlie and Possum
Turkey and Jack
point grey muzzles to the sky
sniff the wind
their names as elusive as dingo spoor
scatter in gritty vowels
around you the tall basalt corridors
echo to wild dog notes
elegiac, untranslatable.

Boreraig

Mantz Yorke

Above Cill Chriosd, I pass a roofless four-square
house and steadings, then ascend the grassy track
where rails once carried stone to Broadford's pier,
skirting spoil-heaps, a winding-wheel's remains,
and the quarries abandoned when cold calculation
proved their superior marble too costly to extract.

I contour round Ben Suardal, squelching across
marshy ground to the bealach, then down
Allt na Pairte to Boreraig's abandoned homes,
imagining how hard the living must have been
even when potato and herring were plentiful,
for famine was always coiled beyond the firelight,

awaiting the moment to slither in and apply its slow,
unrelenting squeeze. The silent ruins castigate
the displacement of crofters from green glen
to bog and stony littoral, to the preferment of sheep.
Sound economics by the landlord, for one shepherd
was cheaper than a dozen families – a reasoning

with power sufficient, a century and a half ago,
to allow the discriminate use of bayonet, truncheon
and the firing of homesteads, with locally no wood
to reconstruct burnt roofs. Ethnic cleansing,
of a kind. I think of the old, the young and the sick
creeping back to sleep in windowless outhouses,

pierced by cold on a winter's night, some to die;
and their neighbours, fearful for their own fate,
unwilling to help or dare to challenge the Church's
proclamation that eviction was the will of God
and a chance for the ignorant to repent their sins.
But what sins? Occupation, not legal documents,

had always given rights to land. Appeal to law
was set to fail: incoming lowlanders, made special
constables and justices of the peace, understood
fully what was expected – to prosecute with zeal
the landlord's 'improvements' with no consideration
for the dispossessed. I leave this desolate glen,

scrunching along Loch Eishort's pebbly beach
and round the point. A squall is draping a grey veil
over Bla Bheinn and bursts on me more quickly
than I can regain the car. The wind wails in my ears –
a belated coronach for the long-departed –
and flings hailstones against my stinging cheeks.

Background

Ann Egan

Land is everywhere about us,
uneven line bedraggles borders
familiar as our palms' turn.
Nothing will wear away

the depth of its possession,
soil's sweetness is within us,
we came from it.
We want to tend the clay,

hunger to possess its stretch,
know it will be our possessor,
rooted in our background.
Behind symbols of our status,

clay trickles fine as spider's silk,
tough as tendrils of a creeping plant.
Sift of soil through the close

link of our fingers
marks us in our own place.

Welat

Cemalettin Cinkilic

Ax welato ez rêketim
Behna axa te dur ketim
Çaxa navê te derbas bu
Agir min ket ez vêketim
Hey welato ez ciwanbum
Bo te jiyana xwe derbasbum
Dijmin xwest ruhê min bistine
Ez nave te derbas nebum
Welatê min Kurdistane
Xemla Mezra Botane
Hatiye parvekirinê
Nav Ereb, Tirk û Farisane
Çavê welatê min şin e
Yek Urmiye yek ji Wan e
Boy azadi û serxwebunê
Hemû Kurda serhildane

Country

Cemalettin Cinkilic

Ah my country, I set out away from you
Left behind me the smell of your earth
When your name was mentioned
I caught fire, burned down

Hey my country, I was young when
I gave up my life for you
My merciless enemies wanted to murder me
I didn't relinquish your name

My country is called Kurdistan
The jewelled treasure of Mesopotamia
It has been taken over
By Arabs, Turks and Persians

The eyes of my country are blue
One is lake Urmiya, the other lake Wan
For my country's freedom
Every Kurd is a warrior

Thirst fugue

Barbara Cumbers

after 'Todesfuge' by Paul Celan

They hold the land in the dust of our houses.
As dusk falls they bring out ancestral maps
and command that we follow their lines on the land.
They command that we wait at their checkpoints,
they heft our worth in the steel at their belts,
they trap thirst in the iron of their gates.

A man farms the land you once owned, Khadija,
he waters your mulberry tree from clear pools.
He herds us in rubble, makes dust of the wells.
Remember the clear pools, Ibrahim.
Thirst is a settler in Palestine, he takes and he takes,
he stands at his checkpoints with iron,
he commands that we wait in the hot sun.

A man studies old maps in the strength of his house
he sets lines on the land, he builds walls around water
he covers our crops with ashes. Your mulberry tree, Khadija.
He pipes the rain to his houses, thirst is a settler in Palestine,
he daydreams of Zion, he strips us at checkpoints,
he commands that we wait, he commands, he commands
that we walk for our water. Your clear pools, Ibrahim.

We dig graves in the dust of our houses
thirst is a settler in Palestine he shatters our wells
he shuts gates at checkpoints he takes and he takes
he lives in a strong house with his tanks as dusk falls
he makes us wait as he daydreams in iron
he herds us in rubble
thirst is a settler in Palestine

your mulberry tree Khadija
your clear pools Ibrahim

A child asks the river

David Olsen

> *Why does your flow not fill the sea?*

Until now I've never filled the sea.
With constancy I've fulfilled
complacent faith in endless equipoise,
balanced flows enriched with upland silt,
and borne the weight of melting snows.

But now beleaguered ice retreats;
its shattered shards shall rend
hubristic vessels plying here
and there in bold titanic pride.

Now, as seas begin to rise,
and floods engulf the lands you till,
I blamelessly deny your accusing eye.

> *Does anger flood our homes and crops,*
> *and drown our herds and flocks?*

The floods are mountains' tears,
rising not in anger, but in sorrow.

> *Why in sorrow?*

Like mothers everywhere, I say:
Ask your father. He should know.

The woman in the moon

Carol Ann Duffy

Darlings, I write to you from the moon
where I hide behind famous light.
How could you think it was ever a man up here?
A cow jumped over. The dish ran away with the spoon.

What reached me here were your prayers, griefs,
here's the craic, losses and longings, your lives
so brief, mine long, long, a talented loneliness.
I must have a thousand names for the earth, my blue vocation.

Round I go, the moon a diet of light, sliver of pear,
wedge of lemon, slice of melon, half an orange, onion;
your human music falling like petals through space,
the childbirth song, the lover's song, the song of death.

Devoted as words to things, I stare and stare;
deserts where forests were, vanishing seas. When your night comes,
I see you staring back as though you can hear my *Darlings,*
what have you done, what you have done to the earth?

The taming

Mary Jean Chan

The heart is a forest
that many have tried to tame.
Sometimes it's the incessant
humming of insects that
bothers them, teeming
in the water, soil and air,
too easily killed but too vast
to ever be crushed. Other times
it's the way the wind sifts
through the undergrowth
overturning jagged pieces
of rock to expose their
smooth, taut underbellies.

Once it was simply the way
the air was pungent with
loam and leaf and light
that made them stop
in their tracks like deer
blinded by headlights,
only that the deer would
die because of the lights,
and they knew they'd die
for want of it.

Those who have tried it
will tell you that there is
only one way to tame a forest.
Abandon your fingers at
the forest's edge – the life
that throbs through the trees
is too strong for the chipping
away of bark to matter. Mobilize
armies of steel and flesh
fusing till steel-tipped
fingers pry the arteries
open at the roots. Start

building roads of concrete.
The undergrowth's
too heavy with life,
so you have to choke it
with something
it cannot possibly digest.

Greenies

Cath Drake

They won't fool you with their dazzled, stupid eyes.
This world is too sharp, too shiny, too hungry
for those who hide in greasy ecology centres
setting their weedy underwater vision on the takeover.
Climate change has their grubby fingerprints all over it.
They've got hedge funds in Antarctic ice blocks
and those wretched almost-extinct creatures.

They collude with trees and grass to creep
into everything like triffids shooting into windows,
smothering homes and choking computers.
So keep building car parks and tower blocks,
drive cars back and forth over thick black bitumen,
gather great horned bulldozers to clear forests
and their barricades, banners, their grovelling songs.

Dump insecticide over whole hinterlands from space
and knock out as many species as you can.
Create huge tracks of salty desert, inject rivers
with wastepipe cocktails, then shop faster
than China can make stuff and create mountains
of fermenting landfill where plastic bags blow forever
and an acrid liquid seeps deep into the ground.

Grab them at parties and tell them what you really think:
they peddle the hues of slime, of the worst monsters
and come from a mouldy planet darker than moon-cheese.
They want our buses, stop signs, bridges, cathedrals,
everything to blush with moss until there's nothing
but their awful colour spreading and infecting,
and birds and deer grow giddy in the thin naïve air.

Message to our world leaders: stop recycling

Selina Nwulu

'History repeats itself first as tragedy then as farce' – Marx

So I'll recycle,
change my light bulbs,
buy bags for life, travel local
I'll become Friends with the Earth
and together we'll ride *The Wave*,
and throw placards at towers of power
I'll develop a zest for all things green,
plunge my hands into the soil below
and let its properties sustain me

But only
if you
stop recycling
Stop.

Stop
recycling your lies,
our hands tied to half-baked rhetoric
that gives rise to our demise
Lies
Surrounded by oil drenched pen pushers
Who subjugate and perpetuate the pain of
the people below
Our people below
Stop
Stop recycling,

Tearing apart our communities
Now empty Shells from the mess you've made
drilling, fracking, and attacking
The earth below
Our earth below
Stop
Stop recycling,

Because we're choking,
over-consumed and undermined
Land- grabbed, dignity lost
losing the invaluable from your gain
Stop
Stop recycling,

Because we're dizzy
cockeyed from the spin
from your thirst and your lust
for yen, dollar, sterling
Stop
Stop recycling

Because we're weary
of your biofuelled deceptions
Your loopholes and propaganda,
corruption and barefaced slander
Stop
Stop recycling

Let's make this a real *Fair Trade*
I'll do my part
and you
try something new
destroy dusty rhetoric
throw it away, throw it to waste
take pride in starting again

Stop
Stop recycling,

Twelfth Night

Reclaim Shakespeare Company

BP: If oil be the fuel for us, drill on;
Give us excess of it, that, surfeiting,
The planet may sicken, and so die.
Let's drill again! And cast a dying pall,
O'er the tar sands of sweet Canada,
The Arctic and the Gulf of Mexico,
Stealing and screwing over.

RSC: British Petrolio! By the roses of the spring,
by branding, sponsorship and everything,
I love thee so, that, discarding my pride,
nor wit nor reason can my passion hide.
For I do love thee for thy patronage
With adorations, fertile tears, with groans
that thunder love, with sighs of fire...

FESTE: If this were played upon a stage now,
I would condemn't as an improbable fiction!
Alas, poor RSC, how hath BP baffled thee?
Thou hast made contract of eternal bond
With a notable pirate, a deepwater thief!
Art thou mad, to profit from such a dissembler?
For some are born green, some achieve greenness,
And *some* purchase a semblance of greenness by sponsoring cultural events...
I prithee, RSC, direct thy feet
Where thou and BP henceforth may never meet!

RSC: Enough! No more!
Oil's not as sweet now as it was before.
BP, thou villain! How was I beguiled?
Disguise, I see thou art a wickedness,
Wherein the oily enemy does much.
You spread a green and yellow melancholy,
Sitting without conscience in your offices,
Smiling at grief.

I would I were well rid of this knavery.
Out damned logo!

To the miners

Sofia Buchuck

Named after Joseph,
The Mine is in the north
Of a country where exile became known.

Desperation grew each second,
In the Earth's womb
The miners begged for air, food, water,
The miners begged for life-
To all the forgotten gods,
Of this universe.

Never were candles lit with such devotion,
Fathers and mothers waited,
Children and wives waited,
The whole nation waited,
The world waited.

Life and death danced night and day with their heavy silence,
The thin country of Chile,
Has been torn since birth,
Is lawless for the workers,
Lawless for the poor,
Blind to their Indian brothers;
Orphans with faces of clay,
Storm fighters in the Land of *Lautaro*,
Where sunlight is made of purple dawn

After all the wars and injustice
See them united by torture
Standing shoulder to shoulder,
For the heroic miners,
Bearers of gold.
Born to die,
Before they reached forty,
Some before they were four.

But the Mapuche lie down tenderly,
Place their ear on the Earth.
hear the cry of Pachamama-Mother Earth.
They left the heart of denial
Went on hunger strike and the Kultrung sang
With the voice of children dashing like moonlight
All over the world.

The Machi saw the smoke,
Songs of resistance and the poisoned stream;
The mountain asked the eagle,
And the eagle agreed, there was no time to wait.
The miners embraced their injured mother with all they were made of.
To feel the unseen bleeding veins
And the mouth of the sea spat angrily,
Shamed by Earth's victory.

Mother earth rose up,
Like the peasant rises each day,
Gave birth after sixty days of heavy waves,
Not only to 33 men,
But the flourishing spring held in buds.

The women stayed there praying quietly,
Hope was fragile,
But sometimes as strong as an Araucaria tree.
Men and governments were powerless, Before
the magnificence of stone.
The women sat side by side,
Day after day,
Waiting for the breath of life to return.
To reach the breath of life Once again,
To re-live birth,
Like never before!

Exile

65

Anne E. Caldwell

It came to pass,
that Cain slew Abel
among the sheep
grazing in the fields.
He slew him out of spite,
out of fear, a
need for something
that was not his.
Or so the story says.
It says that G-d threw Cain
into the world –
a mark placed upon him,
so that all would know
what he did.

But Cain did not leave –
he has not been thrown out.
And his son
has grown up believing
that the sheep grazing
in the field beyond the
olive trees
were his father's – always.

Frontiers

Chrissie Gittins

The Elsinore strawberries hung in their syrup
like air balloons in a red sky.
Seville orange slivers, marinated overnight

in Jameson Whisky, lay cross-hatched
in gelatinous amber.
Carefully wrapped for the flight,

they nestled in my rucksack,
refugees from my overweight case.
But they were not allowed –

they might be explosive,
the percentage of liquid to solid too high.
I pleaded their case – presents for my host,

home-made. *That's worse*, they said.
Would you like them? I asked the young woman
who tried to be kind?

Not allowed.
I'd like to think, at the end of the day,
when no one was looking,

she reached in the bin of disposed of possessions
and rescued my jars.
I hadn't lost my clothes, I hadn't lost

my childhood in photographs,
I hadn't lost my country.
And still it cut me to the quick.

As the plane lifted from my country
I thought of you fleeing to the border
with your life, only knowing

you were near to the camp
when you woke in the jungle
to the barking of dogs.

to convince her suitcase Vilma packs for Prague

Kerrin P. Sharpe

she had never enough dresses
to save her Jewish father
never enough shoes
to forget the trains

she had never enough rope
to harness her coats
never enough belts
to hide the smoke

she had never enough
in the old Czech way
to clothe her father's ashes

or open the dark wedge
of his stable door
to the sad eyes of snow

Instructions for behaviour at border control

Harry Giles

Wear a red dress. Paint your eyebrows green.
Ensure your gait mimics the gait of a lion who's fallen
awkwardly from the sofa and is pretending he hasn't.

Hop sideways and shifty across the line that reads PLEASE
STAND HERE. Throat lustily *Now you see me Now
you don't*. Drop to one knee with a ring made of luminous

plastic and zebra-skin. Ask the loneliest guard to marry you.
Stroke her gun. Whisper precisely *I studied witchcraft*
then grin because with your green eyebrows they can't but know

you are telling a truth. While stamping out hours of queue,
gamely ignoring the teeth of glossy instructional vids, invent
a Magnificent Teleportation Device, and with its tachyon trails

write theories of history to gut the future. Return, steaming,
and sing of this to the queue and the guards and the screens and the signs
till the thrice-damned terminal implodes from the singular weight

of its own internal contradictions. And breathe again. And spell
again the teleportation device, the manifesto, the implosion.
Make a lever of your time. Handle yourself with care.

Asylum cocktails

Keith Jarrett

> *Supreme Court judge Lord Rodger, ruling that UK asylum laws will now protect gay people's rights to live without fear: "male homosexuals are to be free to enjoy themselves going to Kylie concerts, drinking exotically coloured cocktails and talking about boys..."*

I (Your Disco Needs You...)

On the weekend, I seek asylum in the arms of some Kylie
remix the DJ spins in the club night called Exile: concerts,

in summer, wellies wedged in muddy fields, and drinking
too much; it all now feels too frivolous, like the exotically

priced bottles, wasted again on the dance-floor, coloured
now with its spillings. Time again they ask what cocktails

of pills I'm on tonight. Maybe it's my wide-eyed stare and
my hunching, my pockets, full of hands, doing the talking

for me. I shrug through lines at the bar. I guess I'm about
done with these places, these tiresome rites, these boys.

II (2 Hearts)

When the airplane and sky lie
parallel, your body does concerts

with your heart; it throbs like drinking
too much. Tell them your exotic ally

sent for you. Passport coloured
too dark to stay without cocktails

of stories they'll check over; and
-roid customs officials keep talking

evidence, they say fear is about
ticking boxes & not boys loving boys

III (Reprise: All the Lovers)

I should be so lucky if I could publicly *slow* dance
with the man I love in my parents' homeland.

Where they're from, bodies burn for less:
even a rumour can be a passport to the next
life; or the next dismissal; or the next head-

line. And *I just can't get you out of my head*:
denied the right to stay and deported, next
to more news about benefits. But this is less
about who should have the right to this land
and more about how our double-standards dance.

Citizenship test

Ken Evans

If you smile when you're stopped and empty your pockets
For the officer who stopped you last night
    You're one of us.

If your sister dances with whoever she likes
Whenever she wants and you don't sit late
In the kitchen listening
    You're one of us.

If some of your best friends are white
But you don't bring them back to the folks,
If you know the metres of cloth it takes
To wrap a sari, the total of suras in the Qu'ran
    You're one of us.

If you're sure we'll score the winning goal
In a penalty shoot out semi-final,
If you can recite three Shakespeare sonnets,
Two soliloquies and the ending to Cymbeline,
    You're one of us.

If you know enough Pashto or Urdu
To order a pint and packet of crisps,
If when you hear someone say on the bus, 'I'm not racist
But'… you turn and refuse to accept their caveat
    You're one of us.

Dust

Simon Miller

Joseph – he wears that coat like an oily skin,
The pockets deep enough to hide his life in
Threaded with a sediment of old dust;
Sand carried from that other world
Which endures now in a windless heat
Acacia and cattle-thorn and ochre stone,
Continents of time from this cold shore.

From the dirty shelter on the promenade,
Pungent with piss and weekend drift,
He watches the ceaseless ocean flow:
Grey-green slabs lift, dissipate or heave
Dropping solid and angry against shingle.
He watches a gull cutting lines across
The sky, charting a long journey home.

Sometimes when the liquor drained
He could sing a throaty song of women
With weeping smiles and feet that
Stomped a red-dust pathway through
The grass clumps to his compound,
If only someone here could respond
If only there was still dust to pound.

Maybe the rain

Kate Adams

How will it happen? Which day?
In her garden I try to forget.
Never hot for long in England.
Maybe the rain come
filling a sky full of nothing
and the sun will struggle.
If you been hungry you remember
when your pocket was empty,
no way on the bus
and the car you dream of
was for someone else.

When they coming? Warm day
or freezing? My road yellow, black
in shadow; asleep under the snow;
England, never my country.
Some letter fly through the box.
I know one word, *refusal*;
hurts, like a friend give me poison.
All that waiting, for their decision,
years in a room, dirty, a prison.
I say, *Good luck, let them try and catch me.*

She is talking to her flowers, my *English*.
I ask, *Is it possible.....?*
She deaf to me.
If you have house and passport
you remember your holiday
not this foreign brother.
Gold in the garden of England
but here never hot or yellow too long.
She look at the sky, *Maybe the rain will come.*

What is it to be detained or

The single seeker

Osama Ahmadani

It was raining outside,
by the door lied an
umbrella
looking at me, then pointed to the door
I felt alone!
Although my
friends scattered around
my flat, I pulled
the cover and picked
a book,
I spent that night reading
For the hundredth time
things fall apart.

Junk mail

Brian Docherty

Like everyone else, I turned this into a verb.
As mistakes go, this ranks with Francis Drake
sailing past the Golden Gate, or Decca Records
turning down The Beatles. I threw it all away.

Six of these things offered to change my life.
I read & discarded five; the important one
slipped straight into the bin unopened.
A week later the police kicked my door down.

If you've ever wondered why the Home Office
is so called, or who lives in the Home Counties,
I'll tell you; not for me, or anyone like me.
But it was my home; now I am a Resident Alien.

Not in Surrey, but in the country my parents left
when I was three. I don't speak the language,
I dress different, I walk different, I look different.
I am not a tourist, I am a displaced person.

There is no local equivalent of Marks & Spencer,
no Charity Shops, no supermarket, nothing
to help me be anonymous. Now I know that
'straight off the boat' feeling, am truly alienated.

Only the petty-bourgeoisie enjoy the luxury
of useless information; if you're poor, or rich,
it all matters. School in London didn't prepare
me for this. Now my education really begins.

The prayer labyrinth

Ruth Padel

She went looking for her daughter. How many
visit Hades and live? Your only hope
is the long labyrinth of Visa Application
interviews with a volunteer from a charity
you're not allowed to meet. You've been caught:
by a knock on the door at dawn
or hiding in a truck of toilet tissue
or just getting stuck in a turn-stile.

You're on Dead Island: the Detention Centre.
The Russian refugees who leaped from the fifteenth floor
of a Glasgow tower block to the Red Road
Springburn   Serge, Tatiana and their son,
who when the Immigration officers
were at the door, tied themselves together
before they jumped – knew what was coming.

Anyway you're here. Evidence of cigarette
burns all over your body has been dismissed
by the latest technology. You're dragged
from your room, denied medication
or a voice. You can't see your children,
they're behind bars somewhere else.
You go on hunger strike. You're locked
in a corridor for three days without water

then handcuffed through the biopsy
on your right breast. You've no choice
but to pray; and to walk the never-ending path
of meditation on *not yet*. Your nightmare
was home-grown; you're seeking sanctuary.
They say you don't belong. They give you
a broken finger, a punctured lung.

Mahdi Hashi

Stephanie Turner

Terror! Terror! Where are the terrorists?
Better lock them up! So we can be terror-less!

Mahdi Hashi is just a baby boy when the civil war breaks out,
his family seeks refuge whilst swords clash and flash at the sun.

We go to school together, eat chicken and chips for lunch.
We pass paper notes with Keith and Kofi during class.
We share a moment's silence when the bombs hit the twin towers.

Terror! Terror! There are the terrorists!
Better lock them up! So we can be terror-less!

Mahdi Hashi is a BRITISH-Somali. Mahdi has earned his citizenship.
The Mayor of Camden awarded him certificates, a social carer and a youth
    advocate.

The MI5 have never questioned me about why I leave my country.
The secret services have never warned me not to go and see my family.
The MI5 suspect Mahdi Hashi to be an Islamic extremist.

Terror! Terror! Hashi is a terrorist!
Better lock him up! So we can be terror-less!

What has he done? Who cares, he's on the terror-list
'Matter of National Security' says the home office.

Mahdi Hashi is being questioned again, the MI5 want him to be a spy.
They take DNA, fingerprints and his name. He is warned not to leave the
    country.

The Home Office have revoked his citizenship. The UK has left him stateless
over *allegations* of *links* to *some* Islamic Extremists.

Terror! Terror! Hashi is a terrorist!
Better lock him up! So we can be terror-less!

What has he done? Who cares, he's on the terror-list
'Matter of National Security' says the home office.

Mahdi Hashi has been detained, tortured and forced to sign confessions.
Mahdi Hashi has been missing, he appeared in a New York prison.

Terror! Terror! Who are the terrorists!
Better lock them up! So we can be terror-less!

How do we know which ones are the terrorists?
Those who have witnessed know what terror is.

You were welcomed to seek asylum
then you were abandoned and left to be hunted
for not becoming an instrument
of their political war.

M

River Wolton

I

Someone had come with her
to show her the way

but they didn't know her name,
her mother tongue.

Even before I heard it
I could see her story

in the way she didn't smile
or frown or say Hello

to our eager Hellos.
She looked through us

as if we'd brought her here,
thousands of miles

from her three children
and the streets she knew,

Sheffield January
imposed against her life.

Even when we pointed –
tea, coffee, milk, sugar –

spoke louder, lifted
a make-believe cup to our lips

she said nothing after nothing
and yet I couldn't stop seeing

the men who had taken
and sold her.

Then someone arrived
who spoke her language;

as they talked
there was no mistaking

the rifle
lifted to the shoulder,

there was no mistaking
gunfire.

II

In the time it takes me
to learn Hello *Jambo!*

in Bajuni, she learns
a hundred English words,

how to find her way
down London Road

along Fargate
to this church hall;

she enrols in class,
goes to the shops,

befriends Jawi,
smiles.

Today
she shakes my hand

and says *I like here,*
I like to watch TV

copies from the flipchart
in careful script

Where do you feel
at home?

Returning home

Sofia Buchuck

My mother stayed between borders,
Brushing the long hair of memory.
She tells me everything I missed since my departure.
She cures me without request,
Baths me with chamomile, Matico herbs,
then she puts flowers on my head.

My mother has an altar between the mountains,
Teaches me how to speak with winter and silence.
She knows the wild herbs that once saved a troop of ancestral explorers.

She knows the roots of this forest well,
Showing them to me as if they were nothing.
My inheritance is the beauty of my country,
Mother passes on to me.
She smiles playfully before the sun,
Whilst light penetrates the jungle,
Walking me to the trees where the Pustis nest.

She sits me at the head of the table,
Whilst she takes the old chair, which was once mine,
At the opposite side,
Where my other brothers and sisters used to sit,
Now my eldest brother sits quietly.

She cooks her best recipes,
Served with the cutlery saved for celebration days.
Today is supposed to be a happy day;
And we cheerfully glance happiness in the shine of our eyes.

My feet had kissed the land where we were raised–
Eating raindrops.
Between candles and colorful days,
With the songs of crickets and parrots flying up the sky.

Mother cooks in the woods,
And smoke fills the sheets and curtains,
With the smell of poetry.

I feel the red and grey heart of my father
Absent and in exile.

Yet, the bells play once again,
A final dance of arrival.
I am in the moment,
Ready to welcome my brother, sister and their children,

The ones who had not returned in 25 years,
Whilst my white-haired mother waited without complaint.

All tempests have ceased,
Alien victories, sometimes ours, All had passed,
Births, marriages and deaths.
Mother still waits between the fine lines of borders,
In our oldest place with the smell of home.

Five Broken Cameras

After the film by Emad Burnet

Kate Adams

When it was over we watched *Five Broken Cameras*.
I did not know what else to do. The priest, the flowers,
the coffin were unreal. What was real was you
and me on a bus next day, his empty place,
snow on the hills, sleety rain and no one knew
that he and I were your *Article Eight* and how
he tried for you although he was ill.

So we watched *Five Broken Cameras* that afternoon.
You preferred *The Terminator*, not this *sad movie*
about the olive groves, the encroaching wall,
blood in the dust and building again,
each camera, a window, a witness to pain.
He came to court, a witness for you. They said
we were not your family. You said, *He was part of us.*

The roots go deep even when everything vanishes.
As you waved goodbye from the top of the bus
I saw those Palestinian boys facing the soldiers.

War

City

Jennifer Brough

A sea breeze carries salt
to the wounds of women
bowing at the wall
with scarred hearts
and families in rubble.
Words fall out their murmuring mouths
and drop like stones at their knees
on streets paved with ancient texts
that pulse with every detonation.

Yellowed pages fly amid dust clouds
as scrolls unfurl from the hills
draped like streamers
over children's arms,
their eyes wide as prophets'
wise beyond their realm of shells.
Skeletons dance atop the concrete ring
wearing ragged flags of black, red, green and blue
eating up warm prayers of mourners.

Across the waves,
headline drones hover
over printed tower blocks
whose rubrics twist and shift
with digestible lexicon
served over coffee and bacon.
Are they neutral newspapers? that plaster the public
on subways, sidewalks, screens no bigger than a finger,
rebuilding all wreckages
to compact messages
and inked statistics
tattooed on the conscious
for less than a second
before a host of tired typefaces
drag their inky heels
across blank sheets.

When the sea sounds calm, the wall
sleeps between all that is seen and heard.

Day of the dead

Marina Sanchez

Some bleached, others jutting,
but most are still in the dark.
When rain seeps through
our honeycombs, we are laid

bare, by rivers and roadsides,
in woods, pastures, olive groves
and orchards, around cork oaks
and fig trees. We lie scattered,

tied, blind-folded, bullet
casings among us: men,
women and their unborn.
For more than seventy years

we've watched the visitors,
they are less hurried now,
no longer afraid; the women cry,
leave flowers, try to cover us,

the men still throw handfuls of earth
over us, bow. The boys who came
with them are men now, who stand,
watch, ask openly to lay us to rest.

Fragments for Ali

James Byrne

lend me a single syllable
from Assyrian cemetery ash
from the ashes of Ishtar

unruffle my birdsnest ignorance

                Ali

you who brothered me there
like a son and bronzed silver
into figures of amity

in the desert path above Tartous

              through salt tides
              and toothsucking sand

the bell of a single syllable

                Ali

      *

hardbreathing of pebblestones
                          promises
              lost to the iron-shore sea

the upturned hulls
            of fishing boats
                      wet with life

                  as if hope had struck
                      suddenly
     and was bundled out by the sun

      *

winter ices the weathervane
ditch-lilies
     in the Alawite district
where your ailing mother lives –
        reproach of the tank's eye
    death-chills
        tingling the museum gates

and somewhere beyond the pocked wall
and somewhere beyond the General's spyglass
among shelled-out new builds
and frail city stanchions

     your son walks
       the herded miles

    *

blood in the jasmine
sweat of death
    ....
    ....
how do new buds grow
from beheaded flowers?

    *

families hide out for months
      in their homes
insomnia-riven
    betrayed by the dark
      and the painted
    irreality of television

relatives names
     on blacklists
in windows   purloined
    of the old familiar faces

*

where in the Mallajah hills
is the lamb of your niece?

     sorrow of the olive grove
     bones that conspire in the Queiq river

to speak is a game of chess

terror in the telephone
where no-one appears to listen

        dread of breath
     silence that roars

*

an amphitheatre
     laboured over
brick-by-brick
     now cordoned

where the villagers
     cannot be sure
of the informers
     from the mob

school-less children
     stare out from
pillars of rock
     to the distant

grey Mediterranean –
     mesh of Europe

Blood moon

Anthony Levin

'Hearing news of the war [far away]
the leaves of trees were burnt.'[1]

slaughter in the streets

The moon will never
again be white, like us
      blank (effaced)

We, the gang of bystanders
Watch the streams run out
Out to the lunar seas.

'Abba! Abba!' a young boy shouts
with his arm hung across the street
like an old friend, his dusk eyes
still twinkle-twinkling on the ground
playing notes from a forgotten song–

---

1   Line from a traditional Punjabi song. Source: Punjab da lok sahit (Folk Literature of the Punjab), SS Bedi, Navyug, 1968

Srebrenitsa and Ratko Mladich

Vincent Berquez

The mistakes were created
when the sun was asleep
and the light kept hidden
the mishaps in a greater
silence of a settled abyss.

There were no witnesses
to speak to yesterday
when the rubble was cleared
and the victims were in rows
on a bed of bloodied dust.

The mistakes were created
when the day was alive
and the night did not expose
the murderers to the victims
lying in homes like tombs.

There were witnesses
who will speak out today
as the rubble has been cleared
and now a murderer
is exposed for the world to see.

women in war

Eleanor J. Vale

we wait with our babies
by the methane lake

for bubbles to rise
and give us peace

for how can they grow
and not be told

yet how can we bear
for them to know

how their fathers
spray semen

as savagely
as gun-shot

Reapers

Samuel Tongue

The cockpit is a hive under the Nevada sun.
Everyone sweats. Vegas burns on the horizon;
a man loses a million, slams his glass down, makes a million.
A coyote picks at the trash on the edge of the base.

The pilot's chair creaks as she sits, heavy and pregnant,
her belly pushing at the console. Her feet are swollen.
Her sensor-operator is young, remote; he pushes into the cockpit –
'Hey guys, what motherfucker is going to die today?'

They circle the village six thousand miles away,
somewhere between Baghlan and Mazar-e-Sharif.
Nowhere. It is night. The warm stink of goat rubs against
the sweet smell of young pomegranate trees.

The picture spots and flickers – switch to infrared.
The sensor-operator watches,
fixes the scene with his gorgon's stare.
It is night and it is hot. He studies the screen.

The cameras are programmed to pick up
typical militant behaviour, suspicious movements,
gatherings in the night. White heat signatures,
people eating inside houses, moving along the dark road.

A mother and father are making love on their flat cool roof,
white heats merging in a rising thermal.
The sensor-operator is expert in decoding
whether an embrace is a stranglehold, a covert kiss, a bite.

They close on the target; a small goat-hovel,
dark against the hill. They hover, the crosshairs buzz red,
the pilot fires. Countdown from ten.
At five, a child blurs inside the shed.

32-inch flat screen TV set

Jasmine Heydari

Blast after blast shakes the tall living room windows in the middle of the night
and the X-shaped duct tape pasted across the glass performs another dance.
My imagination goes wild: emerging from behind Nanna's black leather couch
and every Dracaena plant there is now an armed man

But this isn't the time for tears.

Pots of white orchid flowers break;
the gasoline lamp falls from the wooden shelf,
leaving an unwanted trace
and the smell of burned flesh and hair penetrates the air.

This is the moment when cries of pain become trapped inside my five-year-old
ears.

How dreadful! How terrible! people exclaim
in rare moments when I let a detail escape,
revealing a past I do not wish to tell.
Fascinating story though, they say, and I smile politely...again.

I think to myself, *fascinating* is not the word someone
once trapped under a pile of bodies would ever say.

'Tell me more,' my friend says.
Remember, I whisper under my breath, to him war has never been real.
For what are drones and missiles, to those who have never lived in their fear, if
    not just another construction of words, neatly composed in a set?
In the mist of envy, I wish for a delete button, wish that I could rearrange

and erase, erase, erase
the image of an empty eye socket, black smoke, flesh torn away
and buildings tumbling like my nephew's lego pieces.
Awful, poor you, poor child, they say.

My reply is not what they expect:

Shit happens. It was a long time ago. Who cares?
In the fear of breaking the norm of politeness, I hold back and never say:

If you too had smelled burnt flesh and ran among ruins of despair
then you would know that sometimes we simply need to forget.

And some things are best unsaid.

My mother and Nanna whisper prayers to a force mighty enough
to put an end to all horror and fear during another ordinary raid.
This is the door inside my mind I do not wish to open or revisit,
although I'm fully aware that it is still here.

Azizam, gerye nakon, kamkam hamechi dobare khob mishe.

Posttraumatic stress was what they labelled my lack of concentration during
    class
Mother cried, Nonsense!
My daughter is just fine, I will not hear of this again!
No need for *you* to pee in your pants or be irrationally scared of sounds.

After all, we are now in the comfort of the West.

Years later, when I describe
the pear shape of the gasoline light
and the blue colour of Nanna's emergency get-away bag,
the one filled with food and water supplies,

Mother shakes her silvery head and says: Erase, delete and excel, my child!

The past is in the past – and yes there was a war and people died,
houses crumbled and you lost a doll and some cousins and an uncle
who used to put you on his lap and tell you stories of a far faraway land,
but whom you surely cannot remember now!

Eyes fixed in the air, she places her flowery teacup on a coaster with dancing
    dervishes,

and says: Now listen, today there are other wars being fought,
other sirens waking children in the late hours of the night, but for you,
let war be confined to that 32 inch flat screen TV-set;
let it be another image, let it be just another word.

There is no use in remembering the bad, no use at all.
I cannot help but agree with her.

But then there is the sound of firecrackers and fireworks
and me jumping in the air with nothing but irrational fear –
as war is just another word of consonants and a single vowel,

still a door is standing ajar, somewhere.

As I join in the laughter of another New Year's celebration or just another
    National Day,
watching the black sky go bright with colours and sounds like thunder filling
    the air,
I remind my mind, to calm down my beating heart, that still lingers in a past
    that is no longer here.

Before we crossed to Timbuktu

Mark Fiddes

Mamadou was as light as chaff
I wheeled him round the whooping circle
Of his friends as we all came to believe
In the flight of boys

Around us gulls spun over mud spits
Slicking into the sage thick Niger
Fanned with rainbow pirogues,
Washing lines and bleached plastic

We collapsed dazed as late bees
Still breathless, we exchanged gifts
A cowrie shell for a new pencil
Empire red and sharp as a grenadier

Mamadou leaped up and ran over
To the militia man in fatigues and flip flops
Who had all our bribes and booze
And stuffed the pencil down his AK47

Today the crossing is a TV news report
Torched by Medievalists from the North
If he's alive, Mamadou's a soldier now
Or a student, long since flown away

Lord's Resistance Army

David J. Costello

They said he was twelve.
The one with the machete for a smile.
The one who brutality
liberated from restraint.
Its abandonment an undemanding task
for a child.

Betrayed by routine
their abduction was easy.
Three young Aquarians
attired in tribal brightness.
Conspicuous.
Compliant.
A blade at each throat. No
movement save the
earthquake in their eyes.
And at each ear a whisper:
'Don't scream when the knife comes'.
The face.
As personal as it gets.

I listened as the tremulous mouth
recounted its mutilation.
Another harrowing in a
place disfigured
by our colonial knife.

Children

No school for children in a time of war

Esther Kamkar

> *O wind*
> *O Childhood*
> *O bridges of tears*
> *breaking under my eyelids.*
> *—Adonis*

Her mother told her
not to carry anything,
not her toy and not her book,
that her hands must be free
to hold other hands on the walk
in the dark, among olive trees.

Now, in the sand-swept camp,
with sand in her eyes,
on her eyelashes,
and more sand
under her fingernails,
she draws with her finger
on the desert.
A house, or a stone?
    Who has the key to her house?
Is she practicing her alphabet?
Her name?

O Little Zainab
with no bells on your eyelids,
       I wish to tell you Adonis
       I know by heart –
           Even the wind
           wants to be a cart
           pulled by butterflies

But it is not the soft breeze
under Damascene September sun,
but samoom, the poison wind,
the killer, sweeping through
the land that has dumped
a man at the gate,
who wants to buy Zainab
from her father.

The forgotten ones

Tracy Davidson

Orphans. Maimed ones. Not the pretty able-bodied ones
celebrities fly half-way round the world to adopt.

A little girl makes her way outside on makeshift crutches,
her left leg gone, right foot amputated, the leg
ending in a misshapen ugly stump.

It looks red and sore. She hasn't got used to the crutches yet,
and they're a little short, so her stump keeps bumping the ground.
Infection is likely to set in. She might lose more.

A teenage boy, so nearly – but not quite – a man, stares moodily
across the yard. Both legs gone, one arm hanging lifeless at his side.
He watches the other boys play football. Playing as best they can
with their various combinations of missing and mangled limbs,
one who's sightless but follows the ball through sound,
another with shrapnel lodged deep in his brain. It will work
its way through until it kills him. But he's smiling now
and whooping, daydreaming of the World Cup.

A charity worker comes to the door to watch, needing a break
from nursing those too sick to play.
She blinks back tears, trying to forget the baby boy,
just four months old, who died in her arms during the night.
She hasn't been here long enough to harden her heart
and accept that sometimes death is kinder.

An ambulance enters the compound, making her look up
and the children pause in their games.
Two stretchers are lifted out, the thin blood-soaked
blankets showing what parts are missing beneath.

The nurse sighs and calls to her colleagues, break over,
and wonders for the umpteenth time: 'When will it end?'

Superman's son

Bestin Samuel

Appa was a Superman
He fought the entire Sri Lankan army with his *chinna* army.
Not because he loved fighting,
But they were threatening to take away our land.

We lived in the forests
I would help *appa* and his friends sometimes,
In digging up landmines.
He told me it was a game adults played.

Many of our *annas* died during fights.
Appa would send me and *amma* to a small house in a faraway village
When he knew a big fight was coming.
It is there that I once saw Superman on TV.

Amma would cry when she saw the dead bodies, but *appa* never cried.
He would just look away in a somewhat angry expression.
I wanted to be like *appa* when I grew up –
So I would also try to do it, blinking away the tears.

Then one day I saw him very worried.
He told us that the Army had surrounded us, and this fight would be very bad.
I was not afraid; I knew he would be safe.
He was my Superman.

But they killed my Superman – blew half his head away.
I screamed, and cried till I fainted on the cold floor of the Army camp.

They gave me food, and let me watch television sometimes.
They asked me where the others were, and I said I didn't know.
They asked me if I loved my *appa*, and I said he was my Superman.
They asked me what my ambition was, and I said I wanted to be like *appa*.

Today they gave me tea and samosas; I like samosas. Also biscuits.
Then one of them came and sat down next to me.
Asked me if I wanted to take a walk outside.
I was happy to, because I hadn't been outside in a long time.

I knew I was about to die when they asked me
To stand still with my back against the boundary fence.
I was silent and smiled a little at the one who asked me for a walk.
And I stood very, very still.

I felt three, four, five shots cracking into my shirtless upper body.
And I sagged and fell down.
After all, I was no Superman.

chinna: small
appa: father
amma: mother
anna: elder brother

A lesson with children

Kathryn Lund

the day Gwen and Osh decided once again that they could share
was the day I told them about Syria
only I didn't use the name or anything like that, or get political on 5 year olds,
    but we did
learn a new world that day, or at least

we learnt the meaning of one. we learnt about children who picked one toy
    and carried it, walking

all the way to where they were safe; and when they were walking

did not argue over whether its name was Pineapple or Miss Lemoncake, or
    spend
some secret minutes taking the paper floors out of their sisters travel house.
    these children,
we agreed, in solemn voices, would be happy to share. We learnt the meaning

of Refugee.

And other children

I told them, have never heard of toys at all. this was greeted with a silence more
    solemn still
and, after those long seconds, the testing by the smallest voice, of whether it
    was true.
These children, we agreed

wouldn't argue over the naming of one small, plastic dog. All the way between
    Lancashire and Wales, with the car packed round them full
of toys from a grandparents loft they had contested
ownership as bitterly as warlords. Now, in the thoughtful silence at the gaping
world they both looked at each other, and removed
hands from their long contested turf:
we remembered the meaning of a word that day. If only it was practised
in a few more places on earth.

Jason

Laurice Gilbert

He stands with his arms crossed,
right hand buried in his left armpit
through the neck of a ripped
two-sizes-too-big t-shirt,
wearing shorts that might have been
cargo pants in a former life.

Beside him his little brother
bows his head to his hands
like he's working at a splinter,
though his eyes look up;
a look not as perfected as Princess Diana's,
but with the same sly effect
of innocence and shy disclosure.

Big boy Jason, though, is up to the task
of observing the observer.
His head turned to the left, eyes right,
his bare feet firmly grasp Wewak –
the rubbish dump he calls home.

With his number one haircut
keeping the lice at bay
and scoliosis hidden
by the baggy t-shirt,
he defies the fiercest challenge.

Starting school at age six –
when he could stand up –
he walked a year later.
At eleven years old
he knows he's cool:
'Mi yet laikim skul!'
Cerebral palsy holds no power
over his advanced education.

The throne

Nabila Jameel

He hits me hard on the palm of my hand
with the stick, for not saying
'Salaam, Molvi Sahab'.

I sit in pain, blinking back my tears
so no one laughs. They're all looking:
I open the Qur'an and recite.

He disappears after Saima leaves.
Zenab says that he takes out his brown slug
which slowly grows,

his beard twitches
and his eyes roll up as he breathes fast,
half-naked in the Wazu area.

We're chanting words of 'The Throne'
His throne remains empty for a long time
but like God, he's still here.

We're reciting verses that instruct
distance between man and woman,
man and girl.

*Wazu: ablution

Like water

Simon Williams

I have seen the plate,
a thin sheet of titanium
perforated at the edges
for screws to fit it
to a fine small skull.

It looked like a map;
a section through
that part of the world
I have to look up
for any familiarity.

Between the white teeth
of the Hindu Kush,
the Swat is uncompromised,
moves away, joins other rivers,
one day finds the sea.

The photos are small,
but I can see the way she shines,
Malala, the way she pushes
at the banks when spring comes
with the swell of meltwater.

Patio

Pat Borthwick

You can tell the silence is temporary
as Naresh lays down his hammer
on a sandstone slab. Time for water.

That chip chip chip, tink   tink   tap,
sometimes the sound of a chiselled split
creaking in a larger block

along a fracture line, ricochet
around the deep walls of the quarry
and set concentric rings trembling.

They'll never escape the rim of his tin cup.
Jewelled veins glint among slag heaps
under a sun too large for the sky

to hold it up. Then, just as the echoes start
to fade into somewhere a bird might sing,
the klaxon blarts and Naresh, his face

furred with dust, picks up his tools again.
Thwack. Thwack. Thwack.
Even chipping the tiniest hole

wakes his baby brother. Shwick, Shwick.
He harvests the landscape, each slab measured by
the length of his bare feet. *Better than school!*

He and the others are sure of that.
Their strikes drown the growl of wagons
as gears clank through the gradients,

puffs of chalk-dust rising from words
scribbled on their tailgates. *Liverpool,
Hull, London*. Words Naresh will never

understand. There's more important things.
As he works beyond day, the night quarry
is alight with a galaxy of tiny stars.

(A)typical Cairo street kid

Kaamil Ahmed

He's not your average Cairo street kid.
Instead of begging, poking, prodding
then sticking his hand into your pocket
and fleeing, with anything
you were stupid enough to leave
in it, he just sits there.
In the doorway of a closed bank,
head leaning on the threshold.
Most of time sleeping.
Well, maybe not.
It's hard to tell. Eyes droop,
body limp, sapped of energy.

I'm forced to wonder;
does he not beg because he's hungry,
or is he hungry because he won't beg?

A potato

George Roddam Currie

Am I dead yet Mama?
No my child, you are not dead yet.
Mama, it is cold in this train and wet and dark and noisy and smelly and scary
And I am very hungry.
Ah, my child, all I have is a small potato.
Here, come and have it

When will I die Mama?
Ah, my beloved child, it will be soon and soon and soon.
What is death like Mama?
Will I have all these pains and be cold and wet and hungry and smelly and
    afraid?
No, my child, in death you will live forever.
Death has no cold, no wet, no darkness, no noise, no hunger, no suffering, no
    fear.

Mama, Mama, will I be hungry for potatoes?
My Child, you will never be hungry again.
I promise you that–never, never, never.
You will never be hungry again

Oh Mama, Mama you make me so happy, but what are those rivers in your
    eyes?
Ah, my child, they are rivers of water to wash you with my eternal love.
But Mama, Mama, I have a big love for you but my rivers have no water.

Am I dead yet Mama?
No my child but here comes Uncle Josef who will help us to die.
Now we have to have a shower.
Oh Mama, there be water just like in your eyes.
And Mama, Mama, will Uncle Josef have some potatoes?
Yes, my child, he has many potatoes.

Am I dead now Mama?
I am not cold, not wet, not smelly, not hungry, no pain, no fear.
Yes, my beloved child, now you are dead
And one day all the people in the Universe will know about you and your
    children.

Mama, Mama, will I have children now that I am dead?
Oh yes, my child, you will have many children.
When the rivers of the showers and my eyes wash us into the earth
To make rich the soil for all eternity
All your children and your children's children
Will be a potato.

Dead babies

David Lee Morgan

Imagine living in a city about the size of London populated entirely by babies. Imagine living there for a year and in the course of that time watching all of the babies starve to death. Thirteen point three dead babies per minute on average. Seven million babies a year. Dead from starvation.

You've got food. As much as you need. Enough for everyone. For all the babies. For everyone. But they're babies. They're helpless. They can't feed themselves. Only you can feed them. And there's only one of you. You race from baby to baby. You sleep only when you collapse with fatigue. But there's seven million babies.

Thirteen point three dead babies per minute. An hour TV show would last for eight hundred dead babies. You could even that up to 1k per hour – naturally you would even it up to the next highest number since the basic groundswell of starving dead babies is always increasing. In the music industry, you would call that – seven million with a bullet.

Maybe we could put it on the stock exchange
The Dow Jones index.
The Hang Seng index.
The Dead Baby index.
This poem is fourteen dead babies long.

Sentenced

Amjad in the sky

Ryan Paterson

Amjad stared at his feet
All African violet with mud and dust.
Amjad glared at the sky
Pretty clouds looked down with pity.

Old blood sat under his finger nails
Young fear trembled through his hands.

His 'tendencies' still lay in the heart,
Lay in the streets, on the fruits of the markets,
Lay in wombs and schools and elders.

After. Wrists bent, bound and eyes swathed
Whilst the crane spits out its noose
Like a slimy, slim tongue.

Then, up to the sky and closer to God.
Up there the wind makes his hair dance.
His Adam's apple imploded,
His neck snapped like
A tree splitting.
His screams attempted escape,
But the rope mutes and gags.
Even the right to cry out is caged.

His feet kicked in the quiet,
A feeble rag doll in the sky.

The blindfold then fell from around his eyes
Gliding down to sit with the crowds
Who stared up in horror at the skies
Next to the clouds the dying man hovered,
'He flying' whispered a small child
Whose Mother leaned forward to cover his eyes.

With only a noose for him to wear
Amjad stared at his feet kicking the air.

The kestrel

Jaki McCarrick

In memoriam Troy Davis

On the morning they kill Troy Davis
the air outside is still and solemn.
Birdsong is unremarkable
and I think of yesterday's kestrel.

My neighbour had seen it descend
on a pigeon gorging on worms
and scraps of bread laid out
by Anne who lives three doors up.

He said that watching the feathered frenzy
was Maurice, my cat, who, prominent
under Anne's hedge, seemed transfixed
by the sight of a bird killing a bird.

Yet Maurice and I both know –
though it's me who needs reminding –
that everything is prey, and that instinctively
each species will not protect itself.

And though they prayed in Georgia,
a man still walked to his dying
where others of his kin had come
to swoop and hollow him out.

Stone the crow

Stephen Miles

No more,
the stadium purpose,
football,
friends, neighbours,
men and boys,
anticipating,
baying,
the truck arrives.

Standing,
here,
while you peer,
I watch,
you leer,
motionless,
without conscience,
entertained.

Words fail,
my numbness,
shame, guilt,
you, we,
are not human,
this is not,
god's will.

Too late, to save the crow,
save your arm,
save your stones,
give her a bullet,
for her,
me,
you,
for god's sake.

Chinese kidneys

John Daniel

Apparently the Chinese use criminals' kidneys for transplants.
Rich Americans pay $40,000 dollars for fresh kidneys
The kidney donors are marched into a stadium
wearing yellow jackets like road workers
young unemployed men roaming China
guilty of theft or drug-dealing.
They kneel down,
hands behind backs,
the cord tied round the throat
so they don't make last-minute speeches
against the State.
A bayonet is pushed into their back
so the body stiffens
then they are shot in the head.
A plain van drives up
and the kidneys are taken out immediately.
They are fresher than American kidneys
a doctor says proudly
The wrong-doers are repaying their debt to the State,
which is building a new wing
to the hospital with the profits
white-tiled, luxury
unheard of in China
with en-suite bathrooms
for visiting patients,
just like America.

I imagine the video reversing,
the young man kneeling upright,
the bayonet being pulled out
the backward march to the stadium
for the speeches and harangues,
the young men returning the stolen goods
and then stopping, going in search of their kidneys,
finding the customer sitting in a bar
paying the $40,000 back,
the American saying,

OK bud, it's yours,
and picking up the dinner knife
he carves out the kidney
and hands it back, soft and round as an egg
and falls forward over the table
just like the one executed.

the other side of appearances

Mandy Pannett

this leaf
this small cupped leaf
whispers a soliloquy

about its heart
which is a pitcher trap for insects
dissolving in green cells

dark as a vivid triptych
when both its wings are shut
dark as prisons

where forgotten men
bright as robins or a red-fur fox
turn into pelts

To the men of Guantanamo Bay

Alyson Hallett

(after Neruda's 'The Poet's Obligation')

Today I will not be angry. Instead I will tell you how the
curious pigeon sat on a chimney pot at dawn, his apricot head
bobbing from side to side. I will tell you about grey clouds
massing in the sky, the time I took to lay in bed with a mug of
tea, the stillness and safety of morning unfolding around me.
the radio was on and music danced around my room. The
presenter described the sound of a bassoon as fruity, as if the
player was tasting cherries and apples in the notes he played. I
will tell you again of safety, of opening my eyes and not being
afraid of the walls of my house or the streets outside. Such a
small thing this morning, this feeling inside that makes me
want to seize a piece of gravel, a blade of grass, the rough skin
of your hand. At seven o'clock the news replaced the music.
Three men committed suicide in Guantanamo Bay. But today
I will not be angry. Instead I will take this morning and fold it
into an envelope, beg the birds in the sky to carry it across the
vast blue ocean and press it to the window of your prison.

The wall

Miriam Davies

A tall grey line's been drawn between
ancient river, warm sea
concrete thick as redwood trees
land cut like fatal injury

The lion and the unicorn
mean I can pass straight through
The man next to me has an eagle
it means he stays behind

I talk to the guard in blue with the gun
he's nineteen, like me
same generation
feet in different countries

It means the old lady with white shopping bags
struggling back up the hill
next check point, next chance
tomorrow same again

It means everything slowing right down
life moving through thick oil
oil that spits in friction's heat
and burns willingly, wild

It means where there's a gap
it's climbed through
It means where there's a space
it's drawn on

More than two sides to any country
More than one way to feel free
It means tired footsteps on red Earth
under ghosts of olive trees.

The firmament, La Picota Prison, 23rd January 2013

David Ravelo
Translated from the Spanish by Gwen Burnyeat

A gift for Sigrid Rausing

Nights, so many nights
That I do not see the firmament.
It will be full of stars, I think,
Or the moon with its radiating glow.

I imagine the clouds drifting
Visiting and embracing the stars and planets,
I think of the woman I love,
But what is immensity like?

Is the night dark or bright?
Night dies as dawn approaches
Day is born with a halo's splendour
The firmament is strange to me.

Night without a firmament
I do not see it but I invent it
The rain dances with the wind
And thunder sounds, like a wail.
Show me what the firmament is like
Because I have not seen it for so long
The sky will be grey or blue
I hope soon to overcome this unjust imprisonment.

The kindly interrogator

Alireza Abiz

I have a kindly interrogator
He's interested in philosophy and free verse
He admires Churchill and drinks green tea
He is delicate and bespectacled
He is lightly-bearded and has a woman's voice
He is polite and doesn't insult me
He has never beaten me up
He has never demanded false confessions
He says: only write the truth
I say: on my life!

Request for assistance

Isha

I'm behind the glass looking out

one day when I wasn't looking
they just slid me in.

the others are all outside.

sometimes some of them come up close
and their noses and mouths gigantify

'Excuse me,' I say,
'they've put me in this test-tube and I can't get out'
'Don't be ridiculous,' they say, 'you're imagining things'

'Excuse me,
you look very nice today,
I do like that dress you're wearing,
they've put me in this test-tube and I can't get out'
'They would never do that,' she says,
'They've always been very good to me whenever I needed a flu-jab.
Your voice doesn't half echo in there'.

'Nobody's thin enough to get into a test-tube'
'What are you doing in that test-tube?'
'She must have done something to ask for it'
'Let her find her own way out'
'These people who climb into test-tubes!'

Tidal flow

Steve Garside

(for Faraj Bayrakdar)

There is a space.
A space
which sleeps between
this seeping becoming
of words
and bristling grass
of afternoons.

The space which hits
this auditorium of dark
flecked light of time
with fingernail tallies
and the hanging gift
'outside'.

I wear the promise of my skin,
I am the numb of numbers –
in silence there's no breath
for questions.

Poem for Nasrin

Pippa Little

You spoke with your body
in Evin prison.
Skin ebbed from bone,
hunger aged you.

Hundreds around the world
stand for you
in fine rain, in heat, in public,
bearing witness with their bodies,

the same photo
of your tired, frail face
held up along the line.

Since you refused silence
we cannot live with stones in our mouths.
Look: in some square or city row
somewhere, right now, a woman
speaks your name and the names
of your children.

At the approach of dieback

Hubert Moore

Ash trees in Europe are threatened by fungus known as Chalara Fraxinea

When the ash groans with the weight
of its leaves and the slippered
voice of a mother or father
comes shuffling through on the phone
in the house you once called yours,

when Chalara Fraxinea
eats at the tree-flesh and the
almost fully rounded life
of a mother or father
is ready to end, then you know

what you've always known, you're
in prison now that you're free.
The ash-tree's leafless: anywhere
in the world you can visit
except what used to be home.

Hanging

Moniza Alvi

Like a raindrop suspended from a twig,
or the flower on the brink

of saying goodbye to its stalk,
history is hanging,

Along with the tyrant
and the woman who murdered her lover.

The countries adhere to the globe – just.

And the day is ratcheted
along all the stages of a crisis.

A day is not a compact thing.
Necks are bullish and vulnerable.

The boulders and the dust-motes.
Hang them.

The sun blinks and blinks
with grit in its eye.

As a child, I picked up my pen
and marvelled

how the ink clung in the nib,
the tiny miracle.

Slavery

Lament

Joel Moktar

Loveless as sandpaper, the boatman's cry
cuts over tar black water, dying
in froth at the harbour wall. First light.

The coarse tremolo of crying waves
and callous gulls break on the wet slap beat
of condemned feet, tracing shivers down

the contours of the morning. Red sunrise,
now shackles scratch like ferrous saws to draw
reluctant blood from flesh and sinew.

When your skin has felt the lash and tear
of leather it cannot forget, long
after blood and bone congeal to clotted

mud, the memory stays chained to the
senses. You will recall the livid scent
of agony and the wetness of your back.

Small voices in the mast's creak and bend. Dark
shapes passing silently into water.

Shot through with metal

Geralyn Pinto

When he stood at the crosshairs
of Pershing Drive and Cruise Street,
he saw them marshalled
row upon row on the great
white wall space of Daw and Sons
(Dealers in Antique Firearms/ Estb. 1860);
caught flicker and gleam of barrels
well-oiled and waiting. Time
was cheap as dead leaves, and he
waded through the wither and sear of it,
muscles rolling, pouched,
and packed slugs beneath the iron
of his skin; and pressed a nose, flattened
on a Louisiana paving-stone, against
Daw's plate glass, warm on the inside
and on the outside, cold.
His breath he bequeathed
to the slate grey of November
which would by dusk begin to feel
more like the bleach and brittle of winter.
He caught the chill of it aching in the bones of his ancestors;
saw warm life frost into cotton clouds picked
with care by deft black fingers which
in their time had pounded mealy meal and
fashioned spears in long-ago savannahs.
A switchblade of wind shaved the skin on
his ribs beneath the steel-blue of his jerkin,
tightening rusted memory
around his chest till it felt
like a hull, planks salt-rotted
on the long-haul voyages
that introduced a dark continent to
a bright new one.
Around him Fall sang
like a cotton ginny and beyond
its whining music he heard

the rhythm and beat of darkie melodies
that tried to keep the pickers forgetful
of fevers in the blood and
cracking whips on broad ochre days
and narrow grey ones.
He strained to hear the koo klung klang
of an antique rifle rejuvenated with three
shining lozenges as a rod slid
into a waiting shaft and an index finger
rested on a crooked knuckle of trigger
Inside Mr Daw's son's son's son's
son squinted into a rifle's sights
while a customer with the bluest eyes
watched with a 'deal's on' smile.
Outside the night sang and whistled
with the sad strains of Dixie Land
and the rip-crackle-whoosh of gunfire
snaking red-gold through dun earth,
and it sweated with the steam of dying horses;
but he was chill as a bleeding
Louisiana tenement in winter.
'Kumbukumbu' the drums echoed
incessantly in the ghosts of dead log cabins
and loosened the slugs in their pouches
so that quiet people walking the intersection
of Pershing and Cruise slid unfussily
onto paving stones, leaving behind them forever
uneaten dinners, half-written letters and unpaid bills,
while the iron-skinned man with
white metal fire between finger and thumb
performed a New Age miracle of turning
Mississippi waters into flaming wine.

Chained

Maureen Oliphant

Gently painting the daisies' leaves,
whispering promises of growth,
hiding the label on the beer-brown bottle
of hormone enhancer.

A face open to the sky,
a trusting summer beauty
and I remember the days,
When picked in profusion

from endless warm meadows,
chaining through from the edge of
the bluebell woods, mingling with cowslip
clover, lady's smock and buttercup

we crouched in a circle,
pressing finger nails into green stems
threading them through
making garlands

necklaces, bangles and crowns
working with warm hands, daisy
heads drooping, gifts carried home
through knee high grass, thistles, dock

and I remember a wedding bouquet
of Transvaal Daisies, yellow and white,
wire pierced stems to hold soft heads
high against a trail of orange blossom.

Clouding round the border,
a silent dance
of small blue butterflies
beside the crumbling path.
Feverfew strewn

Creeping rootstock of convolvulus
branching underground, reaching
over the pergola, threading its way
through climbing roses, clematis,

The lawn, a meadow patchwork
of cowslip, buttercup, clover
and hanging by a gap in the hedge
a chain of daisies

I am here far from home, my flesh raw,
I cannot see the daisies or the sky
Chains have a different meaning now
Necklaces and garlands of black rubber

Shackles

Deepak Chaswal

A bird flying
In the sky
Fell on the earth
Tried to cry

A shepherd
While moving the herd
Heard the cry
Picked the bird
Applied the balm
On the body of the bird
Put it in a cage

When the morning came
With light and rain
The bird opened its eyes
Found itself in shackles
Tried to fly
But could not
So tried to cry
But could not
Because the shepherd
Had cut its tongue
Last night
In a state of fright
When the bird in
Its sleep had cried
'Birds are born free'

Terminals: A – Z

Kathy Zwick

Young troops stumble on the cruel irony
of 'ARBEIT MACHT FREI' in daunting filigree.
Silent birds, silenced soldiers, only shrill
crying Polish winds whipping round the kiln.

Lost Property: The surface-stuff of boot polish,
naïve suitcases, eyeglasses, shoes.
The person-stuff of dental fillings, matted hair,
skin, and then – the other: the lost generations.

Under/through the parabolic gateway
of slave labour misery to fated tracks –
terminal of human tragedy.
January, 1945 – quiet, haunting incredulity.

Emptied Tanganyikan villages, routed Congo ports,
empty hearts, empty spirits, emptied generations.
Yoked cousins, chains clinking, lugging tusks and gold
toward coastal People-Markets. Cargo duly sold.

Spices waft. Livingston's malarial mosquitoes know
sad, dark dhow sorrow crammed in cellars low.
Brass-studded ornate wooden doors hint lust – and –
lost dignity, marred trust, the lost and disappeared.

Incredible terminals of human abuse.
Rough baggage – sordid, shocking, saddening us.
Hushed UNESCO World Heritage sites[1] reminding us.
Found Property: Our eternal shame.

---

1   The UNESCO World Heritage List includes 981 sites.
    Auschwitz-Birkenau was added in 1979. Zanzibar's Stone Town was added in 2000.

Offshore

Simon Miller

The ocean steady-pendulums the boat, pitting your rolled horizon,
The deck writhes with pink and pale flap flesh,
Slithers in tentacle, and boneless fish that fart oil.
Call me Boomsong. Chi. Samnang. But do not call me free.

Once as a boy you turned up a stinking dog, dead for putrid weeks.
Beneath the stench you clawed through then,
You saw the slipping fur collapse with creeping maggots.
Never saw such corruption again, until you slopped aboard this boat.
Knee high in ocean -slime for twenty rolling hours,
Salted skin shrunk to bone by water warm as blood.
Call me Nhung. Soon. Tong. Sien. But do not call me free.

Amphetamines oil your coiled limbs, sinewed with fading dragons.
The sak-yant tapped on your shoulder sighs to
Spirits of another place,
                              Where broad-leaves patched the sun, where
The forest pulsed with paths and shiftless rust-root huts were stood.
A drag-net of desires and necessity drew you;
A sick wife, the gleam of enterprise, first of all, lies.
Call me Manop. Sook. Wanchai. But do not call me free.

For months now, heaving those false debts towards shore, heart-stung,
Cursing the taxi that tricked you through the border,
The trafficker's polite, policed laughter – the slaughter
Of those whose hope or legs gave way, expendable commodities,
Sluiced dead from the deck or slung overboard, dark
Bobbing heads persistent against the silver water.
Call me Nanda. Moe. Shien. But do not call me free.

A tourist beached by gentle surf, on the moon-cast edge
Of pleasure, sees the halogen glow of the shrimper's
Lights and – sighing – dreams all is well with the world.

Sak-yant: ritual tattoos said to offer protection to the wearer, common in Thailand, Cambodia and other parts of South-East Asia.

Traffic

Benjamin Norris

Our footsteps follow wakes. Consider,
each pace through even the kindest streets
has been proceeded by those ships, who
pushed hard, and whipped through kindly straits
with the airs of continental drift. A hold
of the same packed-in humanity we all hold –
                stained with salt, slapped up, cut out –
chains upon their ankle-bones

bruising, generations deep. Still,
we are taught to understand these ills, and
laws leer at historical fault
lines cut in foreign stone.
Boats look different, now

the kindest streets hold plaques
dedicated to our sea-change. Liberation names
bridges, bank to bank, then to now. Slavery sank,
only to shadow a different face: cheeks
                stained with salt, slapped up, cut out
of mountain towns. Now, Eastern girls get caught,
on ships that somehow look more welcome
when the shackles become more subtle.

Vegetable

Kayleigh Kavanagh

Trapped in a darkened tomb
eyes too heavy to lift
pulled from the bed, unripened
unready, unsteady. Manhandled and cleaned off
thrown back into the pile

prepped and pretty, no movement made
false hormones pumped in
dignity dug out
shadows sewn to replace
what was taken, stolen, forced
away from the doll

repackaged and put out
placed to place
no prize

no way out.

Women

The sewing circles

Byron Beynon

A suture on the wounds of landscape;
in Herat, under an Afghan sky

peace was lost as women
drawn together like busy thread

carried embroidered cases,
defiant covers for the words

they'd interweave against
the Taliban sentence of death.

Standing together, shedding burkas,
binding their language whole,

those improvised needles
kept sharp for the healing purl.

Esse – to be (haiku)

Marion Osieyo

To be a woman,
my child, freedom without choice,
language without voice.

Embarrassed

Hollie McNish

At first I thought it was ok
I could understand their reasons
They said 'There might be young children, or a nervous man seeing'
this small piece of flesh that they weren't quite expecting
so I whispered and tiptoed with nervous discretion.
But after six months of her life sat sitting on lids
as she sips on her milk nostrils sniffing up piss
Trying not to bang her head on toilet roll dispensers
I wonder whether these public loo feeds offend her.
Cos now I'm tired of discretion and being 'polite' as my baby's first sips are
    sniffed up by shite, I spent the first feeding months
of her beautiful life
Nervous and awkward and wanting everything right
Surrounded by family until I stepped out the house
It took me eight weeks to get the confidence to go into town
Now the comments around me cut like a knife
As I rush into cubicles feeling nothing like nice
Because I'm giving her milk that's not from a bottle
Wishing the cocaine generation white powder is toppled
I see pyramid sales pitches across our green globe
and female breasts banned. Unless they're out just for show.
And the more I go out, the more I can't stand it,
I walk into town I feel surround by bandits
Cos in this country of billboards hoarded with 'tits'
and family newsagents' magazines full of it
WH Smith top shelves out for men. Why don't you complain about them
    then?
In this country of billboards hoarded with 'tits'
and family newsagents' magazines full of it
WH Smith top shelves all out for men, I can't feed
In case that small flash of flesh might offend
And I'm not trying to parade this, I don't want to make a show
But when I'm told that I'd be better just staying at home
And when a woman I know was thrown off a bus
And another one told to get out the pub
I'm sure the milk makers love all the fuss

All the worry and stress and looks of disgust
As another mother turns from the nipple to powder
Ashamed or embarrassed by comments around her and
As I hold her head up and pull my cardy across and she sips on the liquor made
    by everyone's
God, I think
For God's sake, Jesus drank it
so did Siddhartha, Mohammed and Moses and both of their fathers
Ganesh and Shiva and Brighid and Buddha and I'm sure they weren't doing it
    sniffing up
piss as their mothers sat embarrassed on cold toilet lids
In a country of billboards hoarded with 'tits'
In a country of low cut tops, cleavage and skin
In a country of cloth bags and recycling bins and as I desperately try to take all
    of it in, I hold up her head
I can't get my head round
Your anger towards us and not to the sounds
of lorries offloading formula milk
into countries where water runs dripping in filth
In towns where breasts are oases of life
now dried up by freebies and signs, in labels and logos of gold standard rights
claiming breastmilk is healthier powdered and white
packaged and branded and sold at a price so that nothing is free in this money
    led life which is fine
If you need it or prefer to use bottles, where water is clean and bacteria boiled,
    but
In towns where they drown in pollution and sewage
bottled kids die and they knew that they'd do it
In cities where pennies are savoured like sweets
We're now paying for one thing that's always been free
In villages empty of hospital beds
babies die diarrhoea fuelled that breastmilk would end
So no more will I sit on these cold toilet lids
No matter how embarrassed I feel as she sips
Cos in this country of billboards hoarded with 'tits'
I think I should try to get used to this.

angel on the right

Shamshad Khan

She does her prayers as usual

folds the jaanamaz
the way she folds her wings
the way she folds her dreams

in half
then quarters
and then once more

her refuge
this three foot by one foot
of magic carpet

where she is safe
from unreasonable demands

she invokes surahs from the qur'an
the prophet's words
sayings from the hadith

on the sole of her upturned foot
she has inscribed the word:
'paradise is under your mother's feet'

like a beautiful bruise all down one side of her face
she has inked the prophet's reply to the question
– who in the family should I respect the most

his answer: 'first your mother, then your mother, then your mother,
and then your father'

peace be upon him
he tried to get the message home:
'you are as equal as the teeth on a comb'

she calls on Khadija, business woman and first witness
of the prophet's revelation
Aisha, leader in battle and recorder of many hadith

the prophet was a husband too
she has hennaed his guidance onto the back of her hand:
'the best amongst you
are those who are good to their wives'

calligraphy of blood
dripping down the inside of her thighs
she does not exempt herself from prayers

she salutes the angel on the right
and the angel on the left

oh raqib and atid
God is great

and then she hopes
that the angel on her husband's left shoulder
will have nothing to record tonight

The Indian woman

Deepa Dharmadhikari

Does not smell of cinnamon
Does not have dusky skin
And languid swaying hips
And red henna at the end of Her fingertips
Does not always dance
In opium-induced trance
Either in temples or brothels
Does not always wear a veil
Or tinkling anklets
Or clattering bracelets
Or noserings and toerings and filigreed jewellery
With furling and swirling silk stoles, scarves, robes, saris
All embroidered, enspangled
Tie-dyed, primary coloured
Does not widen Her large, kohl-lined eyes
Does not always titter or giggle or gasp in surprise
Or ride on elephants
While the rajas go on tiger hunts
Does not always die in the fire
Of Her husband's funeral pyre
The Indian Woman
Is not an Exotic Oriental.

The Indian Woman
Is not always poor and oppressed
Abused, ignorant, insular and depressed
Destitute, dying, pregnant, unhealthy
Is not always starving and sickly
With eight children
And a drunk husband
Who beats Her for daring to speak to other men
She is not always a victim of casteism
With demonic gods and false superstition
Who needs Your birth control or sweatshops or amens
Who benefits from Your IMF or devout piety
When You turn Her into a productive member of society
Through your charity

Either by saving Her soul
Or by refusing to drop a dollar into Her begging bowl
Or letting You tie off Her fallopian tubes
As You tell her how Her religion subjects women to abuse
The Indian Woman
Is not a Third World Problem.

The Indian Woman
Does not always cook like Madhur Jaffrey
Always look like Shilpa Shetty
Always write like Jhumpa Lahiri
Always fight like Goddess Kali
She is not always a Bollywood actor
Or a call-centre phone operator
Or a model-minority doctor
Or an arrangedly-married homemaker
Or a sari-swathed mother
Or a Kamasutra lover
The Indian woman is not
What Your fears and fantasies have wrought.

The Indian Woman...
Does not exist.
And yet You persist
To define Her
To deconstruct, deify or demand Her.
Like a doll you can build Your stories upon.
(We Indian women laugh, and walk on.)

I might have left

Kathleen M. Quinlan

that first time, when
his fingers closed around my neck,
tightened, jerked me to and fro.

He was right.
I needed some sense
shaken into me.
Instead I packed
the incident away,
like a forgotten souvenir
of a holiday gone awry.

Perhaps I should have gone when
the glint of blade flashed.
I had a bag by the door, but

no car, no bus, no money. Only
a long snowy road
and a too-thin coat.

none's hands

Shamshad Khan

We were all in it together
so it seems

the ones who tightened the loophole of the law
around my vulnerable neck
your hands are not clean

the ones who read all the reports
and still said it was safe to return
your hands are not clean

the ones who said:
show us, show us the bruises, show us the blood, show us the places he said:
    you will do it or you're dead, show us the scars on your heart and your
    mind, show us the proof that you resisted each and every time
your hands are not clean

we were all in it together
so it seems

the ones who arranged the marriage
ignoring those niggling fears

the ones who heard the bang, bang, banging
but were too polite to intervene

the one who said:
I do
manzoor
manzoor

I fear even my hands are not clean

Cutting season

Richard Scott

After Sara Nason, Nancy and Gertrude.

           the only time a man
will ever pour you tea, whistling
as he unties the black ropes . . .

I am the first in our village
does not want to be cut,
does not want the flat spoon inside of me – they say
all the others knew what was good for them
but if a woman has been cut
her grave is open . . .
           for auntie
they took the iron sheet from the roof
to carve her baby's passage.

Today I climb the bean tree, walk
the well's swollen eyelid, kick
a football
        further than my cousin
but I know they will come for me
for they have given my father
a crate of beer, a cow –
           they will come for me
with the black rope, whistling . . .

Honour

Maggie Butt

Five girls, sitting on the floor in your best
shalwar kameez; emerald, ruby and gold,
clapping to the music, giggling like children
when the camera-phone is turned on you,
covering your faces with Christmas-coloured veils
laughing with your hands pressed to your lips.

I watched you on the news, your glowing clothes.
The camera caught the graceful way you clapped,
then panned to a young man, too close for modesty,
and the story was of a village court, and sudden
disappearances, of punishment for being too close
on video, on the public stage of internet.

How could you know the camera was the
wolf in grandma's clothes, catching you
too near a young man, closing that space
for all the world to see. Its eye too big,
teeth too sharp, ready to rip your bright silk,
soft skin, tear you from limb from life.

Did we not warn you of the wolf, my darling girls?
Not say he might come in with smiles and acid
for your pretty faces, ready to gang rape you for
honour, and that the woodcutter might hunt for you
through all the forests of your mothers' keening
but never find your sweet punished flesh?

You flutter in and out of my mind, bright butterflies,
how you sat close together on the floor in a pool
of happiness. And I search through cyber world
for news that you've been found alive, unhurt,
your innocence intact. But you have slipped away
into the dark hinterland of yesterday's news.

Execution of a teenage girl

Lorna Callery

[for Atefah]

one night
a dark figure
comes into the cell
that stinks of urine

I try to believe
he has come to release me
        instead
he unleashes himself

beats me
where lash marks
burn
red raw heat   pain
forces my legs   apart

I am thirteen
he is an officer
of the Morality Police
they don't believe there's rape

     oh, she was teasing me
     she was not wearing the correct dress
     the hem of her garment revealed her ankle
     that was how she seduced me

I am a threat to society
a bad influence on younger girls

to be sentenced to death
strung up by my neck
in the street

black dresses hang
from black cranes

the metal arm
        cuts angular
        through the midday heat

its claw hoists broken souls
up high into the air
as warning

For an Afghan woman poet

Maggie Harris

Nadia, Nadia. I will repeat your name
to break like waves, a tidal refrain
washing again and again in the wake
of your silenced tongue.
Laugh at the morning, you wrote,
shut the door on the night;
words of hope that cradled
your fear of a place called home
where the blow that felled you like a tree
still flies free.
You were a warrior,
fighting with fists of verbs
etching your right to life
on stolen scraps of paper
the book open at the kitchen table
whilst you stirred the pot
and held your small son's smile.
Nadia. Between us lie continents,
deserts of imagined worlds woven,
spun from dry winds, dust and stones
of a land men stalk.
But even as the heads of the Buddhas roll
their sacred dust implodes, becomes the air
they breathe.
Nadia, you will never be silenced. Names and words are
long forgotten whilst yours rises still,
sing like kites.

Hidden

Barbara L. Lopez Cardona

Hiding underneath a leafy willow,
Her body half submerged in water,
Terror in her eyes,
Pain in her soul
looking on unintentionally, the inert bodies of her father and her mother!
No time for tears!
overcoming all fears
Escape! the only thing in her mind
a great wound in her heart
her instinct of self-preservation
has kept her alive
in spite of dying being her true desire!
she runs, hides changes her name...
trusting in no-one...
not even in the tranquillity of dawn!
not knowing where her footsteps will lead
not knowing whom she searches for...
or whom to tell what she keeps inside,
only vengeance conceals her emotions
placing them in the attic of her soul bereft of speech!
longing for her eyes to become blind
so as not to see so much misfortune...
Despite overflowing in disgust for her enemies
She joins them...
in order to learn their sly ways,
her wish to surprise them
leads her to dedicate her days and her nights to them!
In the quest of the uncertain, in a mud filled road...
she finds no peace, no quietude, no hope, and no life;
she is chained to her memories,
trapped in her past...
she is dead inside!
the enemy has become her,
consumed by hate

she walks the same streets, frequents the same places,
caresses always the same nothingness

She banished her youth… left it tied up in a corner,
she no longer lives, no longer feels, no longer loves!

She is one more victim of the avarice of men,
of an insane war!
a war that kill all hope
that destroys souls.

Mekong women

Sue Guiney

She opens shop along its muddy shore.
  Mango, two dollah. You want?
Sparse teeth.
Dirty nails.
Twisted hair still gleaming black.

Another walks with a French posture,
her head is taller than the length of her back. Her arms
are hooked around her sister's.
  Bonsoir, Monsieur. Merci. Orgoon.

Luring men in by downcast eyes, demure
beneath midnight black lashes. Flashes
of cold escape from their eyes.
The thrust of the river propels.

There is beauty in their duplicity.
There is honour in their slim advantage.

The men slip sleepy heads from *tuk tuk* seats.
The men sleep for us all. It's their right to do nothing.
It's our duty to do the rest.

Power lies in unexploded bombs.

Mother & child

John Gibbens

There's a woman down on her knees down by the roadside.
She's thrown that little white handbag aside
And she's holding on to her child
Where the stones and bricks are piled
And the cars go rolling by despite her grief.

She looks up into the sky that's filled with darkness
And she looks away from Mecca to the west.
She says, 'Every life must end
But, Lord, why did you send
The day when I must see him die myself?'

All the horns are blazing on those passing Hondas
As she brushes down his hair with a trembling hand.
Where the river runs underground
With a distant troubled sound
She'd dipped him in the waters that ward off death.

His father was a stranger and remained one.
On the day his son was born they said he'd gone.
But as the boy became a man,
However wild he ran,
She knew that he was blessed above the rest.

Down the hungry streets on which she raised him,
Guns and drugs had kept the chances slim
And the cost of living high
And heroes in short supply
But he walked a finer line than anyone else.

But they caught him unawares beyond the precinct
And they gunned him down at once to keep the peace.
Now she's holding on to her child
Where the moon shines undefiled
And the muezzin chants to those Carmelite bells.

By the stone that keeps the waters from the waters,
By the holy feet that trod upon that rock,
By the navel of the world,
Into hell may they be hurled
Who sent the boy into the arms of God.

It's the song that you can hear in any nation,
It's the background noise to every front.
By the borders we defend
Show me where Golgotha ends
And the garden where the stone's been rolled away.

Regimes

A crocodile eats the sun

Nick Makoha

The stones on the riverbank have seen you.
Among the tepid reeds you drink the night.

A lozenge of the moon rests in your throat.
Thirst for flesh sweeter than dik-dik fermenting in the gut.

Your nostrils peer through the lake to reveal
the curve of the earth as the world is split in two.

A praying mantis skating along blue mud
knows your secret. Even the bullet lodged

in your right eye can not persuade you to stay
by the boundary. Stones are silent.

A weeping willow has its back turned. The rope
around its waist anchors a wooden boat to shore.

Beside dogtooth violets a soldier's face is reflected
in the rippling glass. A standing portrait ready for war.

You were Idi Amin's teacher? He learned to wrestle
with you in the swamp during the cruel months?

In the shadow of the night with your bodies oiled in mud,
you got a taste of dying, decay and carnage.

wrath was the only nature of God you taught him.
What of mercy, peace and Uganda?

Our bodies still rest in your jaws.

Choeung Ek

Duncan Stewart Muir

We are the noose and the knife and the hook
I am the spade and the shovel, I am the pick
you are the orange earth, your face cracking
beneath the sun.
              But when the rains come
the earth runs red, relinquishing her secrets
of rag and bone.

*

I hear you say that you were absent
and so innocent, but I call you for a liar.
Where you look for difference, for distance
I see symmetry.
              Perhaps you have no blood
beneath your nails, only the mud and dirt
of a farmer fresh from the field.

In your unsown soil, you might raise a crop
of waxed black beans, and suck the sweetness
from each withered pod; or a grove of sleng trees,
their bare white boughs hung with a poisonous fruit.

You might raise a house, a school, an army,
or even just a child who cries in the night
afraid of that orange poison ripening within
each of us, and within himself.

Bilu

James Byrne

Bilu – who gobbled up children for four thousand years
and stalked Dasagiri through the slopes of Mount Popa
booming the great gong of his voice – now folds/refolds
the blue-red silks of his democratic tie (demon-embossed)
and sends sudden felicitations to Venezuelan diplomats,
engineering execs. from the Koreas and the febrile British.

Bilu fleecing the public bank account as he funnels off rice
in exchange for bottle factories (re-forged from the ghost
of abandoned Socialist factories). His children in the North
spray bullets at a blazing jungle, and in the South, (uneaten,
but wholly devoured), they break rocks with their hands.

Bilu addresses the Western assembly in a tongue of whispers,
of how he has reformed from centuries of piling up bones,
while, in the East, a boy lights the matchbox of a minefield.

*Note: A 'Bilu' is an ancient mythological ogre or demon character thought to have
roamed Burma in 2000BC.*

A view of Kidepo Valley

Nick Makoha

The wounded have forgotten their words.
At this hour the earth slows down.

Where their feet once walked my eyes now go,
It is an *old-fashioned dance*, like the tango.

To the fate of a note, they have matched this motion of battle.
The last thing they will remember are ants at their ankles.

That's not a man in pain, it's his body wrestling with the earth.
A bullet to the lung has dislodged his soul to the dirt.

Blisters and punctures are what's left of the body.
Dead goats in the field know this equality.

Tyrants have shown their hand.
These corpses will want their revenge.

From the clays of the body blood now blossoms.
The ruins of our land have become your museums.

For Ben Linder

Dean Anthony Brink

The northern divide sponsors landed men
with gold chains and gloved hands,

men pitched high on pasted billboards
and armed like the brunt of old ships.

Worn rubber soles slip toeing salt lines,
shoddy reserves in the bush bare cartography.

Every maimed and limb-lost feather of justice
speaks to theaters of pressure, harbors mined

to pay the northern tax of goods
to pay off what is not ours or anyone's

but the fancy barking of stiff dogs,
the interruption of ball games,

fires shot in closed offices across borders.
To be nowhere is the safest measure,

and so we juggle and appear from behind
the fine gauze of fluttering flagless drapes.

Kora in Lhasa

Vee Freir

Grey-green uniforms parade
at the epicentre of a culture
they don't want to understand.

The ever-streaming tradition
of paying homage to the giant,
who waits and watches
the Kora –
winding its path
giving praise
to the Potala,
dressed
in its red and white uniform.
Counting mala,
spinning prayer wheels:
Om Mani Peme Hung, around
their sacred palace.

Forcing the channelized course
with triggered guns and averted gaze.
Glazed eyes fixed under military caps.

Loud

Claudia Daventry

The guide is called Sofia. Her name means knowing and she knows
more than a lot of Americans! She speaks English and four other languages
elle parle français habla español si parla italiano ze spreekt nederlands

she was educated at the Travel Guides Academy and by the way
she takes Union gratuities here, in this tin. She's saving. She hopes
to move to the city some day, the block where her mother once lived.
Sofia stops in her village and we get out to have *kofte* with her grandmother
who has two black teeth. Her grandmother can't see. She makes her own
flatbread which we buy. She rolls the *kofte* between her palms. It is raw

but it cures with the red heat of chillies. The grandmother can't use a knife.
She tears parsley with her fingertips: Sofia said it smells loud. She crushes
onion with a wooden spoon and a fist, which makes her white eyes stream.

Sofia says her mother hanged, she swung, she got tallow and greased the
rope, and it creaked as she fell and it broke her weight and her neck
with a jerk.

She tells us she hung from the stairwell in her city apartment with her mouth
leaking black blood and it was this grandmother, she says; it was this
grandmother who lifted her down. She went blind from grief, she says

Sofia's uncles saw them, she says. I think it was Schindler's people. Or was it
Solzhenitsyn and his people. The trains were full as commuterville and their
eyes were coins. The Lubyanka, the monkey wrench they used to wreck jaws.

Sofia wears a blouse with her name machine-stitched on the pocket. I can't
get everything she says but she says it in English again so it's fine. The Union
supplies these uniforms free. Sofia stops the charabanc. We look at a child

crying beside the corpse of a donkey. She is not crying for her mother or the
flies that buzz. We can't hear. We think she's crying because the donkey is
heavy and there is nobody to help her lift it or bury it but we must drive on and

we can't see through the red dust or the yellow splats of flies on the windows
of the charabanc. Someone should send products so they can clean up a bit
around here. We can hardly see the row of men in the truck as we overtake.

They stand. They sway with every lurch and jolt. The washing line cuts into their wrists. Inside each hood it must be, she says, dark. Maybe today they get shot in the head. I tell Sofia: that would be *loud*.

Mr Hu, the executioner

Olive M. Ritch

It is not my decision.
I do not think
about guilt
or innocence.

I do my job –
take aim,
press the trigger.

The fallen body
is taken away – organs
                    transplanted.

Power

Stephen Mead

It's interesting, this electrode they've
stuck in my skull: a switch & needle,
that drug patch to monitor,
control what's considered subversive.
I feel it like a Geiger counter, some
ticking to detect when I think: 'God,
how I love his——'
& then comes the voltage, sharp
electricity keening until numbness
comes on.

Why, in the name of Politics, Science,
should they want to stop who I am?
To erase the spirit, rape the memory,
invade my body with a chainsaw?
Crackle. *Zzzztttt*——
A wireless, in & out, I fade, lose
transmission although
the will's potent still, a quiet
drill of power in the powerless.

That is who starts revolutions,
our energy slumbering to grow
slowly kinetic
like the ocean with its glinting tides,
& also,
like trees, breathing zeniths
rooted as squadrons
in an earth more potent than this
brutal factory of pins, these erodible
shots.

Watch how the waves wrestle, how limbs
flail & surge.
You cannot batten them down now
for I will outlive, survive
this awful ghost state & grow
old, grow old, as the free waves,
the electric Elms sweep
sweep you off.

The Christmas my mother wrote Samwise Gamgee

Yewa Holiday

In December '66, when the harmattan blew hot
dust into the marmalade biscuits,
mother wrote 'Happy Christmas Samwise Gamgee!'
in letters the colour of dried blood on the Morris Minor.

In '67, before the rains relieved the red earth
and the soldier ants jostled
and tramped under the jacarandas,
an election was won but Brigadier Lansana crushed the victory.

Humidity hugged the coast and the ginger
plant smelled of lemons inland at Kenema.
I ate the bark of the cinnamon tree
and sucked goat meat on skewers at Ramadan.

Soldiers wielding sticks and guns collected like wild dogs.
They rolled their words in the recesses of their mouths
and spat them out, 'This way, Madame.'
Their smiles were lines of unforgiving.

My mother drove past their vacant eyes, as the cloying heat rose
from the passion tree and suffocated the bougainvillea.
She laughed in the faces of death's host. Samwise Gamgee
climbed the hill, past the devil dances where once we saw

an angel fall. The Christmas my mother wrote Samwise Gamgee
there was no rain and the colobus monkeys screeched in the sun,
no blood was shed over the fields of rice
and the soldiers squatted like flies in their quarters.

Pyongyang City

Richy Campbell

The ashen path-slabs are free from blemish,
aligned for miles, in threes across.

No-one walks on them,
and between, no-one drives on the roads;

beside, the dark, glass-faced towers
sabre clouds with masts.

Statues of the Kims interrupt the nothing,
their stone feet under bouquets and cards;

underneath, tourist groups photograph each other,
praise brow-raised,

as a khakied guard watches,
waits nearby.

Sometimes the dwellers can be seen:
walking stiff-backed, passing in silence,

clasping small shopping bags
between forearm and rib,

as shadows that haste
from brickwork, pave.

Switch-off:

the illumes in windows fade across buildings,
fireflies crushed in a domino row.

Tonight, the moon slightly reflects
its slight self on glass;

the black of buildings
and the moon's reticence veils,

a blanket that muffles the city
in its fabric.

The 'Kims' refer to the Kim dynasty, who have ruled North Korea since the early 1950s.

Workers

Ashraf's tour of Egypt

Kaamil Ahmed

I'm trying
to keep Ashraf in shot
but out of it, at the same time. Difficult,
from the back of his taxi. Remind myself;
keep the face hidden. Just enough of his blue shirt
and hands gripping steering wheel
but not the face.
Curse the driver's license which swings from its place
next to his tasbih, on the rear view mirror,
with its threat
to whisper identities.

He works as a shop manager,
near the pyramids in Giza.
His government job,
for social security.
He also drives taxis,
to pay for his kids' schooling.
An accountant,
for food.

He wants a middle class. They, Ashraf says,
will help the poor.
Unlike Mubarak's rich men,
who live on their island, in shining towers
which they come out of only during Ramadan
to show their brothers they have food to share.
To tell Allah they care.

Ashraf takes us to the city of the dead.
Where Cairenes live amongst tombs
in crumbling blocks of housing
that clamber over each
other, to reach
for the air of the living.

Welcome to Egypt.

Atacama vigil

Steve Bishop

The world watched the hours stretch
While the Phoenix, fashioned as your saviour,
Plumbed the narrow shaft to inner space,
One man wide, one man at a time.
For a while, we thought you were lost.
But in the certain knowledge of discovery
You created a subterranean world,
Milk, fish and work,
Discipline designed to defy death.

Above ground; Camp Hope.
Everything from tents to t-shirts,
Wives to girlfriends,
Schools, showers and Sky News.
Previously desk bound reporters
Revealed their Spanish speaking skills,
The unknown wives of unknown men
Filled our screens and spilled their dreams,
Copiapo was on the map.

Your chances, slimmer than Chile itself
Frayed at first then strengthened
As the rescue mission tied the threads
Of science and solidarity to your resolve.
Slowly, the earth returned you,
Sunlight shocked and embraced,
Sounds unfettered, shook and exploded,
Survival was sucked in with every breath,
Celebrations erupted on Chile's streets.

Only the mining bosses kept their heads low;
What price the price of copper now?
What price the rush to squeeze dry desert
Just a little harder, dig a little further?
What price the lives of thirty-three?

戴眼镜的老民工
西毒何殇

工地有三四个老头
老得就像是 刚从土
里挖出来

干活儿很慢 一个栽警示
牌的小坑 需要挖一整个
上午 没办法，工头说：
已经找不到年轻人了。

他们很少抽烟
埋头 缓慢地挖
土 他们没了土
地 玉米
被挖掘机碾压在土里
还有一些坟
挪到 更靠近河的
那边

他们从夏天干到春天
整个冬天
都在挖土 我每天都能
见到他们

跟那些爬脚手架干活的
年轻人不同 他们只在平
地上挖土 不戴安全帽
却戴着眼镜。每一个 都
把眼镜

用细绳子绑在头上

我从没用绳子 绑
过眼镜 如果滑下
来 我就用多余的
手 把它推上去

Old labourers with glasses

Xidu Heshang
Translated from the Chinese by Liang Yujing

At the work site, there are three or four old labourers.
So old, as if they had just been
dug out of the earth.

They work slowly.
It takes them the whole morning to dig a small hole
for planting a warning sign.
There's no other choice, said the foreman,
We can't find any young men.

They seldom smoke,
but lower their heads,
digging slowly.
They have lost their land.
The corns
were crushed in the field by an excavator.
A few tombs
were moved
to somewhere closer to the river.

They work from summer to spring.
They shovel earth
throughout the whole winter.
I see them every day.

Different from the young
working on scaffolds,
they only dig on level ground.
They wear no safety helmets,
but glasses. Every one of them
ties the glasses to his head
with a thin string.

I never use a string
to tie my glasses.
If they slip down my nose,
I'll use a non-working hand
to push them up.

Call Coltan collect

Sai Murray

3 010 840

We are sorry but this Congolese number is no longer in current use.
Please replace your handset and dial again.

6 020 220

We are sorry but we are currently unable to find a connection.
Please replace your handset and dial again.

9 210 630

We are sorry but the number dialled is not relevant for UK, US and European
    networks.
Please replace your handset at every available opportunity.

Plum rain

Paul Adrian

Méiyǔ
the six week downpour
does not come.

Cotton season
silent beneath the flags,
spindling prayers

breathed through
lips pursed with needles,
fingers worrying

next year's colours;
Lime Blossom. Prism Lilac.
Plum Rain.

To money

Liang Yujing

Money you entered my soul early, earlier than I could speak
earlier than I learned to stand, to walk and to kick.
Among the junk the elders put before me to test my potential
I chose you, grabbing you tight with my tiny fists – an omen
that I'd be rich, a moneybags, though I was then an infant.
How do I feel now, a poor teacher who is writing an ode to you?
Irony, but that is life. You are still the favourite of my life.

You transform from place to place – in America you're a herd
of wild bucks galloping from Wall Street to banks to companies
to hospitals, with their robust horns against people's throats;
in England you drag your billions of pounds across Thames, so heavy
a weight that almost breaks the back of London Bridge, which is
falling down, every child knows; in Europe you use the pseudonym
of euro, in Japan you are yens we yen for, and in China, in China
you turn to RMB, People's Money, only a few people's –

and can be anything – a knife, a shield, a round coin with
a square hole at the centre, a stone, a seashell and even a dog
tooth. Now you're a full basket of waste paper, or a hollow number
in my bank account, but gold, gold, gold is your eternal color –
you shine like the sun into the darkest souls of the world.
Everybody loves you, while they tag you dirty, those Tartuffes!
You are indeed dirty: a virginal bank lady who went to toilet
without washing her hands got gonorrhea, all because of you.

Yes I love you too, like anyone else, who wants to make you
but is made by you, with ambition to tame you yet is tamed
by you. Almighty Mammon, I know you're a jealous god
that only gives prosperity to those who solely believe in you.
But can't you see? In Canton, forty thousand of broken fingers
are scattered along the Pearl River, fingers of the workers
who toil from dawn to night, 15 hours a day, in the sweatshops.
They save you all their lives, but why don't you save them?

Organza

Selina Rodrigues

Culottes, skirts, hats, scarves of lace and crepe
slip in their polythene sheets like wings.
The tenth working hour in the basement.

No clock, no daylight, one mutters, one sings.
I pause, and my fingers trace a stitch
dropped in Dhaka, a button lost in Beijing.

Swathes of material to dye and print.
A fleeting thought – to rest and be held
by the satin capes or upon the silk bibs.

Clothes piled on limbs, the hundreds buried
in buildings for fashion, but still machines purr
for customers, in fluorescent shop fronts.

What fits – what will I afford to wear
whilst other girls stitch and press in the heat
and we dress in the season's latest colours.

They tend the moleskin and finely-chewed silk,
chiffon, tulle and brocade. Against their bodies
the embroidery floats and then is clipped
and crinkles on our hangers in the high street.

Sewing on jewels

Ali Thurm

emerald like coriander
ruby like red pepper
topaz like moong dal
diamond like coconut milk

My mistress chose me for special work
because, she says, I have the quickest fingers
                              even by moonlight.

Our needles flash like silver fish
darting through rivers of coloured cloth
                              by candle light.

I've learned to sew a fine, straight seam
then cut the thread off with my teeth
                              even by starlight.

each week the big man takes the clothes
and loads his special van
                              by electric light.

We sing all day. We're not hungry.
Daddy has the gold he sold us for
                              by gas light

emerald like coriander
ruby like red pepper
topaz like moong dal
diamond like coconut milk

The maid (i)

David Nunn

Rising before the sun
the shadow woman cleans
with cat-like care
another woman's home

No sound betrays
the soul that grieves
for her shadow family
of unborn dreams.

The maid (ii)

David Nunn

The young woman sits apart
silently mourning her loss
until the urgent demands
of another woman's child
recall her to the present
and with quiet dignity
spirit subdued by her fate
she attends to the whims
of the child who must replace
the one she may never know
and focus of all her love
from unborn to forever.

Unequal

Correction

Eleanor J. Vale

19 year old soccer-player
19 year old kite-flyer
19 year old team-mate
19 year old lover

19 year old South African
19 year old daughter
19 year old lesbian
Zoliswa Nkonyana

Google her story.

Marriage equality (a haiku poem)

Benjamin Hayes

I.

I shouldn't even
have to write this down for you,
but I will. Here goes:

Equal marriage rights.
Two people love each other.
None of your business.

There is no reason
to deny the happiness
of complete strangers.

I'm trying to stay
calm as I write this, and yet,
the anger, it builds.

It is an anger
apropos of such bitter and
selfish rancour.

II.

The Church of England's
concerned new legislation
undermines marriage.

But this is marriage.
Holy matrimony might
still hold sanctity,

If you accept that
religion is bigoted
beyond salvation,

But marriage is not
exclusive to religion,
is not held by it.

If you want to hold
onto your fear and hatred,
you're free to do so.

But you're not free to
impose said hatred onto
the rights of others.

'Do unto others…'
The Golden Rule. It seems to
have been forgotten.

III.

It's painfully clear
a referendum shouldn't
be necessary.

And maybe this fight
is not mine to fight, but it's
not your choice to make.

Equal marriage rights
would only affect those who
actually want them,

The people who now
are having their own freedom
dictated to them.

Everybody else
can sit down, shut the fuck up,
and get on with life.

Untouchable

Jill Sharp

She shines like Lakshmi through the fields –
a gentle stride, arms at her sides.
Beside the houses, stooping her beauty
to the earth, she raises the brimming bucket,
its stench sealing her nostrils. Slurry clings
to hair and skin, but nothing changes
on her face, only a puckering of lips
in silent thanks to Kali
for twenty years of women's work,
this dawn till dusk that's nurtured seven sons;
thanks that she's never known the blessing of –
nor visited this curse upon –
a daughter.

Lakshmi: the Hindu goddess of purity and good fortune.

That's one of them

Jasmine King

'That's one of them,' my neighbor sneered,
At this harmless man who hurried past our door.
But those words that disconnected him,
Had turned him into something to be feared,
And all the resentment I could find,
Was projected onto him,
As if a world without his kind,
Would be an Eden before the fall.

And there was that division into light and dark,
Which can turn a friend into a threatening stranger.
We become like fractured tribes huddled round their lonely fires,
Who fear themselves with fictions of the night,
Convinced that all the evil of the world belongs,
To those outside the circle of their light.

Home alone

Richard Ormrod

They come in three times a day –
home helps, hardly nurses,
with never much to say –
efficient in the business:
getting her up, washed and dressed;
or feeding her at mid-day;
later returning to put her away
again, in bed; locked in
the cupboard of her flat
like an unwanted article;
no-one, not even a cat,
to keep her company;

Each visit is precisely
a quarter of an hour:
no time to listen, answer,
reassure; it's a shower,
dressing, then mid-day meal:
it's easier that way,
that's the deal:
nothing to help heal
the confusion in her head –
just wash, meal, bed.

The TV's always on –
her only 'companionship' –
although her focus has gone:
sometimes she sits at the window
waiting for her dead son,
staring at the unfamiliar scene
she's known for forty years:
but now it might be anywhere,
splintered by her frightened tears;

They let themselves in
then lock up when they go,
so she's 'secure' in her prison:
can't go out in her nightie
on a wet night, as she did before:
they're not taking chances any more
– it might get in the papers –
or, worse still, social services
might feel they have to take her in
and *that's* expensive –
she costs enough as it is...

One day they'll find her dead
– dehydrated in her chair,
or fallen in the hall
that no-man's-land between
the rooms she couldn't reach:

Then, once more, they'll
tidy her away: send in
house clearance, cleaners,
decorators, re-let the flat
and that will be that –
it's cheaper that way.

Athenian democracy

Robert Fieldhouse

Sat in the House of Commons, a minister now debates with no members:
questions of love are subjected to no one who may answer
from a pre-set page

Seductive white pages are thrown through smoggy air, in shapes of
thin, paper planes: they land on the laps of lovers, who hide their
pale faces beneath benches.

Ideology flips through the air, to crash inside the blue mind-tower.
Tribes are reformed to class; the rich caring each other with votes;
other tribes losing their minds.

They bow to the rich in a palace of thoughts; reality invading dreams,
while our society crushes below cobalt blue, fool's paradise;
painted on polluted canvas.

Further below, slaves migrate to a secret workhouse, dark with dust.
The minister arrives to the centre of ideology, a castle built
by the Neo-Norman Liege

Thank you for visiting Deathminster

Robin Runciman

Thank you for visiting Deathminster
We hope you had a wonderful day
Now we're a million pounds richer
With all the fines that you've just had to pay
And don't feed the hungry and homeless
Or you'll just get another big fine
Because here in the borough of Deathminster
We've just made compassion a crime

Free lunch

Srinjay Chakravarti

You'll find them waiting everyday
at the Toll Gate near Farmers' Bridge
in Bengal's Burdwan town

for a free lunch
at five in the morning.

They have to live off the crumbs
from the high table of the Green Revolution –
crones and doddery old men, derelicts,
a few urchins, and local scavengers.

When sealed sacks of rice are brought in
by peasants and sharecroppers
from the nearby villages,

they gather around quietly, gratefully,
right behind the traders and middlemen.

The farmers poke thin metal needles
into the jute sacks, just enough
to extract handfuls of the cereal.

The wholesaler scrutinises each morsel,
tasting it, smelling it, rubbing it;

if he likes it, a deal's on –
otherwise, better luck elsewhere.

But what happens to the sample
that's lying on the buyer's palm?
He doesn't need it any more,
nor does the peasant.

Yet each grain
is worth its weight
in every milligram:
it all adds up
to a square meal.

For the starving poor,
handfuls of debris are enough
for a day's sustenance.

That's why they gather at the bus stand
even before daybreak,
queuing up for the twenty-odd grams of rice
which trickle into the hands of the buyers.

Through the morning,
the suppliants slowly fill up
their plates with their rations:

inadvertent alms
from the daily grind
of the un-free market
and its warped economics.

The mattress

Kate Noakes

we found   thrown out   on street
it difficult   shape   weight
we not move   every day
only when police say

it was clean   park dust
chalk   concrete cover us
grubby   I try   I try
make home   under sky

Luca works   casual
cash   wash up   usual
food   food   is all we think
days nothing   hot drink

we fit it all   sleep here
little ones   so small hear
how long   how long for
hard making home   in door

some people kind kind   kind
wake up morning coins find
baker   left over bread
full dream   fills belly head

angry shopkeepers mean
shout at us   throw things   scream
kids scared   don't know   ask why
making home   under sky.

当年在海口
乜人

一九八九年，六月十日，晚七点，海口街头
忽然发现自己身无分文，却一直在 活着，没
有床却坦然入睡 羡慕一条狗，它毕竟还有饭
可吃 回想起来只是大体上感觉的饥饿 习惯
了空着肚子看别人满桌子的 杯盆狼藉，只是
止不住浑身发抖 在海边打发光阴，无聊地看
着沙滩上的 男男女女，在一栋栋办公楼摁下
门铃，大多数没有人应声

候车室应该是为流浪汉准备的公共场所
我在月台上来回走着，假装我的班车总是
还有一会才到站 保安过来驱赶，赶紧把发
抖的手 藏进口袋。他说如果你真的是 非
死不可，最好是快点！
他甚至跟我长得像，戴着近视眼镜，镜片看上去
也够厚的。我想象他下班后也跟我一样 买两块钱
一瓶的白烧，喝下去焚烤孤独的心 短暂的麻醉会
让人变成不需要吃饭的神仙 早上醒来胃在燃烧，
喉咙说不出话，头重脚轻 后来总算就业，工作是
对付垃圾跟尿臊味 摸着口袋里硬邦邦的几个钱，
顿时觉得 这婊子养的城市又成了广阔天地

That year in Haikou

Nie Ren
Translated from the Chinese by Liang Yujing

June 10th, 1989. At 7 p.m., on a street in Haikou,
I suddenly found myself still alive, though penniless,
falling asleep easily without a bed,
envious of a dog, who at least never lacked food.
In retrospect, it was only a sensation of hunger.
I'd been used to staring at the scraps left by others
on an empty stomach, yet couldn't help trembling.
I idled along by the sea, blankly watching the men and women
on the beach, and pressed the doorbells
at every office building, but seldom got an answer.
The waiting lounge was supposed to be a public place for hobos.
I walked to and fro on the platform, pretending my train
would arrive in a moment.
A security guard came to chase me off, as I hurriedly hid my shivering hands
in my pockets. He said: if you really
want to die, die now!
He looked even a bit like me, wearing a pair of myopic glasses, whose lenses
    looked
so thick. I imagined he'd go, like me, after work
to buy white burn, two yuan a bottle, drinking it to burn his lonely heart.
Temporary numbness would turn him into an immortal with no need for food.
Mornings he'd wake up to find a burning stomach, a dumb throat and a head
        too heavy to raise itself.
Days later, I finally got a job, to deal with trash and the stench of urine.
Fingering the hard coins in my pocket, I suddenly felt
this bitch of a city had somehow turned into a vast land of heaven.

Protest

The demonstration

Douglas Dunn

It looked as if about to become very nasty.
Helmeted, holding shields and truncheons, in riot gear,
The whole, extremely uncomfortable wardrobe,
The police squared up to the students
Who waved their banners and bottles of mineral water.
Some were outrageously got up as fairies,
Not a few in kilts, others like undertakers –
Top hats, tail coats, carrying the coffin of their cause.
Young women flaunted legs and behinds,
Many of them singing 'The Beaux Gendarmes'.
'Bugger this,' said the officer in charge.
'We'll beat them at their own game.'
He passed the word to his second-in-command,
Who passed it on the third, who passed it on
Along the incredulous, obedient ranks.
Then the policemen lay down and the students carried them away.

A Chinese protester in New York

Liang Yujing

A demonstration is taking place at Union Square.
Among the protesters, there's a Chinese.

At a mere glance, I take notice of him.
In a split second, I recognise him as Chinese.

He neither shouts nor talks with others.
In the crowd, he walks to and fro, in silence.

He shows neither anger nor smile,
Only strolls back and forth, holding a banner.

He seems a total misfit in the revolution,
Like a small fish, wallowing in great surges.

One minute, he's pushed to the tops of the waves.
The next minute, he gets drowned in human tides.

But I take notice of him at a mere glance.
In a split second, I recognise him as Chinese.

Not only due to his black hair and yellow skin,
But because his every behaviour looks so lonely.

Loneliness, probably, is the nature of Chinese,
And nature grows from an unspeakable despair.

Although it's in America, in New York City,
Chinese still fail to keep pace with others.

The other banners: Occupy Wall Street!
We are the 99%! Down with Capitalism!

His slogan, two words written in Chinese:
Minzhu! Ziyou! Democracy! Freedom!

Among school teachers

Kit Fan

The gate closed, bell unanswered, basketball court
stripped bare to lines and sparrows.
July is never the month for learning.

A school on Clear Water Bay Road, yet no water
bay, nor road. A bridge, along the scar of a hill
through the Lotus-flowered Magnolias I used to cross over
to the clamour of books.

A month of no children, but the translucent playground
after rain recalls the aftermath of hide-and-seek:
What's the time, Mr Wolf?

The tick-tocking knees,
the run for life. A boy under a tree
restless for the world to spin in ten seconds.

That summer day, among school teachers
we stood and sang.

Not of psalms and gospels but farewell and falling men:
How bodies became mountains.
How the wind knew of sadness, the soil
of love. The colour of blood was the colour of our flag.

In the assembly hall children who knew little of death
had seen images of guns and wounds, a speck
of a person stopping a column of tanks.

It was a clear day but we were all shut in.
The ground deserted to the democracy
of the sun.

The cicadas buzzing their way
to the dead of summer. The world waiting
under some tree.

A thousand souls still singing
in a dark assembly hall on Clear Water Bay Road.

Al Hurriya fi Masr

Caroline Rooney

To gather with poets in Qasr El Nil,
To compose the coming of revolution.
To point out that stapling, not feeding, the mouths of the people
Is not what is called 'stable government,'
To question why Amrika peddles its policies
Through the padding of presidential pockets,
To object that it's this that preserves the despot,
To note how the state stokes its extremists
For they're the excuse to cling and cling on,
To observe the elites ring-fence democracy,
To ask why modernity can't be shared,
To learn that the 'aid' money's a bribe and a tax,
To reveal it's pre-pledged to American arms,
To take in the lack of scope for reforms,
To spend a new day groveling to be,
To get bullied by police and government officials,
To have no medicine for your sick child,
To witness the shrug-shouldered mess of the careless,
To have kefaya then more than enough,
To realize all tributaries lead to the sea,
To see the tide of the real arrive,
To take to the streets,
To take to the streets,
To take the streets,
To pray, oh God, let it be now,
To wrong-foot the rigid with rhythm,

To become a living human poem.

Concrete

Caroline Rooney

Written after the May 2010 IDF attack on the 'Mavi Marmara'

They looked forward to meeting the children when they landed.
The bombed out buildings would no longer resemble abstract paintings.

His bloodied head on the deck, him dead: you ask if the bullets were real?

The soldiers looked like moated towers, human tanks. Tanks look like cowards.
Like metaphors, they recoiled from those they shot at.
A woman wrote on a placard in Hebrew...

EVERYBODY SHUT UP! EVERYBODY SHUT UP!

In Hebrew, she wrote that the dying needed a hospital.
They captured the sim cards saved in their shoes.
The decoy of oil would spew on talkative shores.

In Tel Aviv, they threw eggs at the Turkish Embassy.
In Gaza, they chose flowers and floated them out to sea.

Grândola Vila Morena, 2013

Andrew Walton

A myriad of petals is thrown into the air,
As if in homage to greed and corruption.
We rise up at the feet of our leaders,
They will slip on our carnation revolution.

They will slip on our carnation revolution
We rise up at the feet of our leaders.
As if in homage to greed and corruption,
A myriad of petals is thrown into the air.

Em cada esquina um amigo
Em cada rosto igualdade.
On each corner a friend
In each face, equality.

In each face, equality
On each corner, a friend.
Em cada rosto igualdade
Em cada esquina um amigo.

Millions are singing our tune;
We shudder the seats of power.
We, the masses, are rising once more,
In the spirit of nineteen-seventy-four.

In the spirit of nineteen-seventy-four,
We the masses are rising once more.
We shudder the seats of power;
Millions are singing our tune.

The laughing farmers

Kate Firth

Because they had no power
they had no words that anyone would hear,
so they laughed.

This was their protest
                        their power
                                    and their weapon.

Some would call it madness:
to march for miles
to simply sit on the lawn
of the Chief Minister
and laugh.

Was this a laughter of hysteria?
Or vision
of a genius
who knew
that when your rights are stolen
laughter is a choice
between survival
or defeat?

They could not be moved,
laughing for hours in the sun
to laugh the government out,
for laughter is the greatest triumph
and the greatest humiliation.

Drowning in the unrelenting echo
of hearts that couldn't be bought,
the Chief Minister
became ridiculous.

And for fifty thousand laughing farmers
come election time,
the name of the Chief Minister
remained a joke.

I've never been tested

Phil Barrett

I've never had to silence thought;
to look the other way, pretend
I didn't know what silence meant.

To struggle for, give-up or go without,
simply because of what I am,
or what I do or don't believe.

Never had to watch another's pain,
to make me speak; or suffer
pain to make me talk; seen someone

I love denounced or spoken out against
by so called friends; or to ignore,
pretending ignorance about

where a road or rail might lead.
I've tried to go about my daily life,
speaking out for truth – not just for

friends but strangers too. Yet, untested
by extremes, in this same small world
I've been found wanting and unequal too.

Human rights

Gwen Garnier-Duguy
Translated from the French by Elizabeth Brunazzi

Ce qui est empêché
chaque jour
de notre dimension d'homme
s'enfouit en douceur
dans la mémoire de notre être
demeure là – patient –
jusqu'à constituer le terreau
par où la terreur changera de camp
et s'épanouira en pommier en fleurs

That which is prevented
each day
from entering our human realm
descends gently
into the memory of our being
residing there – patient –
until the moment it becomes the soil
moving terror to another side
where it changes into the flowers
opening on an apple tree

Afterword

Sigrid Rausing

'Darlings, I write to you from the moon', Carol Ann Duffy writes in her poem 'The Woman in the Moon'. It is an apt metaphor. Most of the poems in this collection come to us from another world; a world of pain, of exile, of imprisonment, of alienation.

Reading these poems, I am thinking about the relationship between human rights and poetry. I think of Irina Ratushinskaya's extraordinary, delicate, poems, written on smuggled paper from prison, where the Soviet warders fed her excessive salt and gave her no water, where she spent night after night in dark dank isolation cells underground. I don't want to make reference to the human spirit. But nevertheless: her poetry, which she composed in her mind, helped her to remember who she was. And it helped us to understand the everyday life of Soviet prisoners of conscience. Poetry brings tiny details to life, and in a world where human rights is mostly about reports and abstractions, where real life and real details are lost – poetry can still make us see, and feel.

Here's Jennifer Brough, in her poem 'City': 'A sea breeze carries salt / to the wounds of women'. And here's George Roddam Currie, from the poem, 'A potato': 'Am I dead yet Mama? / No my child, you are not dead yet'. You could weep, for those women, that mother, that child, and perhaps that's all right. We don't have to steel ourselves: our sadness and empathy matter – the ability to feel empathy with strangers, human solidarity, is a state of grace. And reading takes us to that state.

What we know about the Holocaust and the Gulag we know mostly through memoirs and books: Anne Frank and Primo Levi, Carlo Levi, Alexander Solzhenitsyn, Natalia Ginzburg, and many, many others. We know about South Africa from Nadine Gordimer, Alan Paton and J. M. Coetzee. We know about racism, and homophobia, from James Baldwin, and about the Cultural Revolution from Jung Chang and others. I pick those authors, and those situations, at random: there are so many.

Here's 'Shackles', by Deepak Chaswal:

> A bird flying
> In the sky
> Fell on the earth
> Tried to cry

Isn't that also the story of all of us?

Carol Ann Duffy's woman in the moon tells us:

> Your human music falling like petals through space,
> the childbirth song, the lover's song, the song of death.
> Devoted as words to things, I stare and stare;
> deserts where forests were, vanishing seas. When your night comes,
> I see you staring back as though you can hear my *Darlings,*
> *what have you done, what you have done to the earth?*

What have we done to the earth? And what have we done to ourselves? Bad things followed by good things followed by bad things followed by good. Throughout history. So it was and so it will be.

Biographical information

Alireza Abiz was born in 1968 in Abiz, South Khorasan Province, Iran. He studied English language and literature at Mashhad University and Tehran University and is currently doing his PhD in creative writing – poetry at the University of Newcastle, UK. Abiz has so far published three collections of his poetry in Persian. His poetry has been translated into English, German and Arabic and he has attended numerous international poetry festivals. Abiz is an award-winning translator, having translated the work of many English language poets into Persian. He has also written literary criticism and book reviews for literary journals. He currently lives in London.

The poem 'The kindly interrogator' was inspired by my experience of interrogations in Iranian Intelligence offices. The chief interrogator is described here, who was known for being very tough. I knew that he had the upper hand and his report could define my destiny. However, he had a very calm face and behaved politely. As a young student in my undergraduate years, I found him much more frightening than his other lower-ranking colleagues who would swear and occasionally beat the interviewees.

Kate Adams's poems come from her work as a volunteer caseworker for the charity Kent Refugee Help, which works collectively to support immigration detainees facing deportation.

'Five broken cameras' was inspired by the Palestinian film of the same name by Emad Burnat. I watched it with a refugee friend after the death of a fellow worker, someone we were both very close to. The film is an eye-witness account of the continued destruction of a Palestinian village and celebrates the resilience of its occupants who protest and rebuild each time, remaining hopeful in the face of adversity. The film's theme of struggle and transcendence is relevant to the lives of refugees but resonated deeply with me in terms of my own loss and grief. I wrote the poem to honour this.

'Maybe the rain' is about the devastating effect of the refusal of asylum upon the applicant, who contrasts his own unhappy situation with the security and comparative affluence of an English friend. I have used the vernacular of broken English to indicate the fractured existence of an undocumented refugee and the difference in social standing between the two characters. I believe broken English has its own poetry.

Paul Adrian was born in 1984 in Yorkshire, where he still lives. His first published poem, 'Robin in flight', won the 2010 National Poetry Competition. Since then, he has had poems in *The Moth*, *And Other Poems*, *Eyewear* and *Lung Jazz*, and received a commission from the British Craft Council to accompany their Twenty at Twenty exhibition. He is a support worker for autistic adults.

Osama Ahamdani, born in Sudan in 1970, worked as an English language teacher from 1995–9, and then in Saudi Arabia from 1999–2005. He then moved to the UK to join his family. During his time in Sudan he volunteered for the Sudanese Red Crescent, liaising between refugees from neighbouring countries and the SRC to ensure all humanitarian support went where it should. He wrote short stories for Sudanese newspapers, more than 12 of which were published between 1996–9. Prior to this he had started writing poetry but stopped when a dear friend from South Sudan died in 1996. Since moving to the UK he has been involved with many community groups, charities and organisations that support refugees and asylum seekers. Osama holds a degree in English Literature and English Language Teaching from the University of Sussex. He works as an EAL (English as an Additional Language) support assistant at Varndean secondary school in Brighton and volunteers with two charities, Refugee Radio and MIND UK, as a peer support volunteer.

My poems deal with loss, the search for identity and injustice. 'What it is to be detained, or The single seeker' deals with the state of mind of detainees and coping with loneliness.

Kaamil Ahmed is a journalist and poet, who has employed both forms of writing as a means of reporting stories, conversations and observations. The poetry has allowed him to explore issues on a far more personal level.

A few months after Hosni Mubarak was pushed out of the Egyptian presidency, I went to Egypt with a friend and a camera to shoot a documentary about the grievances and hopes of ordinary Egyptians. 'Ashraf's tour of Egypt' was a direct product of this documentary; the subject of the poem was someone we interviewed for the documentary. During the week we spent with him he told us about, and showed us, the effects of poverty and inequality in Egypt. '(A)Typical Cairo street kid' was also a product of that experience. Near our hostel was a bank doorway where every day of our stay we saw a boy sleeping. It was an image that struck me, mainly because the boy's fragility seemed at odds with the chaos that surrounded him in downtown Cairo.

Moniza Alvi was born in Lahore, Pakistan, and came to England when she was a few months old. She grew up in Hertfordshire and studied at the universities of York and London. She has written six highly-acclaimed poetry collections and tutors for the Poetry School.

'The hanging' first appeared in Europa *(Bloodaxe, 2008).*

Phil Barrett, who originally trained as a visual artist, now leads poetry workshops in libraries and schools across north Norfolk. He won first prize in the 2009 Barnet Open and joint second in the 2009 Ravenglass Competition, with poems in the 2010 and 2011 Word Aid Anthologies *Did I Tell You?* and *Not Only The Dark.*

'I've never been tested' was inspired by the sense that 'there but for the grace of God go I'.

Philip Bateman is an editor, researcher and copywriter, living in Cape Town, South Africa. A former Creative and Editorial Director of *Reader's Digest*, Philip has written some 3,000 brochures, mailings, articles, websites and booklets. In the late 1970s he was a research collaborator on the world bestseller, *The Covenant*, with Pulitzer-winner James Michener. Philip is the author of *Pioneers of Southern Africa* and *Generals of the Anglo-Boer War.* He has been the World Champion in Creative Thinking four times, is a permanent MENSA member and Senior Research Fellow of the International Society for Philosophical Enquiry (ISPE), the extreme genius society, requiring an IQ level 20 times rarer than the MENSA level. He has won some 40 international creativity awards and is a Mind Sports Olympiad International Grandmaster.

I wrote 'Guests of Africa' in the dark days of South African apartheid to illustrate some of the complex human rights questions that inevitably arose – particularly in the minds of white South Africans who enjoyed a uniquely privileged existence up to the time of the release of Nelson Mandela and the advent of democracy. It is about a white father trying to answer his son's questions about racial discrimination. The poem raises complex issues that cannot be easily answered and suggests that, at the end of the day, white South Africans may be regarded by black South Africans as guests rather than legitimate inhabitants. While democracy brought South Africa a world-class Constitution and Bill of Rights, it is a flawed scenario and the prophecy embodied in this work is currently being played out through government corruption, inequality of distribution and reverse discrimination – quite the opposite of the visionary democracy Mandela envisaged.

Vincent Berquez is a London-based artist/poet. He has published in the United Kingdom, Europe, United States and New Zealand. His work is in many anthologies, collections and magazine worldwide and his paintings and artwork can be seen in exhibitions and collections. Here are some links to his work: www.wimbledonartstudios.co.uk/artist/vincent-berquez/.

'Srebrenitsa and Ratko Mladich' looks at something that is very current: the desire for truth, justice and peace. Those who are guilty should not be forgiven for crimes against humanity. I believe our attitudes reflected in the media always march ahead, hardly ever stopping to reflect. This poem brings back a conflict of our times that has not gone away but still permeates below the surface on the Balkans.

Byron Beynon lives in Swansea, Wales. His poems have appeared in several publications including *Planet, Agenda, Chicago Poetry Review, Poetry Wales, Quadrant, The Independent, Landfall* (New Zealand), *London Magazine* and *Wasafiri*. Recent collections include *Cuffs* (Rack Press) and *Human Shores* (Lapwing Publications, Belfast). He has been co-editor of the poetry magazine, *Roundyhouse* and was also involved in coordinating Wales's contribution to the poetry anthology *Fifty Strong* (Heinemann), a project celebrating the 50th anniversary of the South Bank Centre's poetry library at the Royal Festival Hall, London. Recent poems have appeared in the anthology *Evan Walters: Moments of Vision* (Seren Books).

'The sewing circle' focuses on a group of women who gathered together in secret in Afghanistan, not to sew, but to study literature, risking death to do so.

Steve Bishop lives in Newcastle upon Tyne and works in the cultural sector in the north-east. He has been involved in international solidarity and human rights campaigns for the past 30 years.

'Atacama vigil' is inspired by the plight of the Chilean miners who spent two months trapped underground in 2010 while the world watched and waited for their rescue. In human rights terms, the poem is about the consequences of economic injustice and the price ordinary people have to pay to support the profits of the mining corporations.

Pat Borthwick is a poet living in the East Riding of Yorkshire. She has won the Amnesty International Human Rights Prize, the Keats-Shelley Poetry Award and the Basil Bunting Poetry Award. She has twice been awarded a Hawthornden International Writer's Fellowship and is currently working on *Open*, her fourth full-length poetry collection. Human and animal rights are always strong themes underpinning her poetry. She is a founder member and former chair of the National Association of Writers in Education (NAWE) and is currently writer-in-residence for the RSPB Bempton Cliffs – the world's largest inland colony of gannets.

'Patio' describes the pressure that young children in northern India are under to work night and day for little wage (and missing school) in order to provide British patio builders with something similar to the golden limestone which has been over-mined in the UK and is now illegal to obtain here, unless imported. Stone from north India is closest in colour and texture to that favoured by the British to enhance their gardens. I believe this is a little-known fact and the more I can broadcast it in the way I know best, the better. Recently, I recited 'Patio' at a reading I had been invited to give, and a man approached me at the end saying that, having heard my poem, he was going to cancel immediately the order he'd just made for some paving slabs.

Dean Anthony Brink is professor of English at Tamkang University in Taipei.

'For Ben Linder': Ben, his best friend, Jim, and I shared a house just north of the University of Washington for a year in the early 1980s. I learned a lot from him and really miss him even now. Since those days (Reagan years) when anyone who cared about social issues was considered strange, I haven't given up. Today, to be American seems to mean giving up power to corporations, who have it; before Reagan, people were still loyal to people first. I try to maintain critical social consciousness and to act positively, as Ben did, to both entertain and better society. He taught me juggling, how to cook, and introduced me to many local groups and experiences with all varieties of leftist organisations in Seattle – from on-campus anti-draft and women's organisations to anarchists far from the ivory tower. But most of all, by his courage, he taught me that life has meaning when we hold ideals of social justice that cannot be denied.

If you don't know Ben's story, here it is in short: he was, by building small-scale hydroelectric dams in rural Nicaragua, helping people who didn't have electricity. He was a big supporter of the socialist Sandinista government in Nicaragua (who didn't trust Ben at first, being an American). Nicaragua had been ruled by a select minority of families who owned most of the land and made peasants of the people and hadn't even tried to develop the infrastructure of the country. Yet the Reagan administration depicted Nicaragua as a 'domino' in the Cold War, and even though Congress denied funding, Reagan's henchmen (Oliver North the most famous) went ahead (this was later known to the world as the Iran-Contra Scandal). A witness who visited the University of Washington after Ben's assassination saw Ben's name on a CIA 'hit list' about the time he was killed, point-blank, after being captured by the American-backed 'freedom fighters' – actually counter-democratic thugs who had sold out to the Americans or wanted the old oligarchy back. Just weeks before, Ben had filed a motion in the US against the US government for funding the war.

Jennifer Brough, who works in publishing, is usually reading, writing or, when she's not surrounded by words, baking and visiting the seaside. She is currently gathering together all her ideas and pieces. In 2012 she won the Royal Shakespeare Company's Writing Competition 2012 and has been published in *Party In Your Eyesocket, Untold Method,* Antlers Press *Invisible Architecture project,* and was recently shortlisted for Virago's Fifty Shades of Feminism competition.

With the ability to report and receive up-to-the-minute information on the internet and social media sites, 'City' examines the way in which words shape events from the point of origin to the eventual recipient. Highlighting the trajectory of words from historic scriptures to rolling Twitter feeds, 'City' examines the function of language and how it can be used to educate, teach and inform, as well as be manipulated to incite anger, sadness and violence. Inspired by the geography of the Israeli/Palestinian conflict, including the separation wall and graffiti as a means of political protests, the images can be anchored in any war-torn country.

Elizabeth Brunazzi is an American poet, translator and essayist currently living and working in Paris.

Sofia Buchuck is one of London's most respected Peruvian artists. A musician, poet and painter, Sofia came to the UK at an early age and dedicated herself to training in her craft, which led to her gaining an MA (Life History research/Hispanic studies) and becoming one of the first people to investigate the history of Latin American refugees since the 1960s. These refugees form an often invisible minority who now represent one of the biggest ethnic groups in London comprising 115,000 Latinos (Queen Mary University of London report, 2009). It also led to numerous awards, including best Latin artist in 2006 and best poet in a foreign language from Farrago Poetry in 2011. She has also recorded many albums and has published her poems in Mexico and the UK.

'Returning home': I returned home for the first time in five years, my previous absence having been 14 years. Living for so long outside your country creates a reality in which everything assumes a different dimension. Exodus, be it exile or migration, causes us to lose an experience and to gain new ones: some of the people and moments we lose are irreplaceable. And the terrible violation of human rights that occurred during those times are very present and visible in my beloved country and my mother.

'The miners of San José' was inspired by the miners trapped in the San José mine in Chile. Created during that momentous event, this poem was also inspired by the great humanitarian support and developments linked to Mapuche human rights that occurred during those hard times. It is also a homage to the victims of Chile's 1970s dictatorship.

Gwen Burnyeat studied literature at the Universities of Leeds and Cambridge, specialising in postcolonial studies. She has worked for Peace Brigades International (PBI) since 2011, and in that time has spent two years in Colombia accompanying human rights defenders like David Ravelo. She has translated the work of Cuban poets for a magazine published by landmark editorial Casa de las Américas in Havana, and writes poetry herself.

Maggie Butt has four published poetry collections: *Lipstick, petite, Ally Pally Prison Camp* and *Sancti Clandestini – Undercover Saints*. Her poetry is widely published in international magazines and has escaped from the page to the internet, choreography, BBC Radio 4, readings, festivals and schools. Maggie is an ex-journalist and BBC TV producer.

'Honour' was inspired by a story on the BBC news of Pakistani girls who disappeared from their village after they were filmed in the same room as a young man at a wedding. Local officials told the court they had been unable to contact the women, despite several attempts, as the BBC's Orla Guerin reports:

> *Pakistan's Supreme Court has sent a fact-finding mission to a remote northern area to establish if four women have been killed, following reports that they had been sentenced to death by a local tribal council or Jirga. It has been reported that the women, along with two men, were condemned when video footage showed them singing and dancing at a wedding (www.bbc.co.uk/news/world-18336983).*

James Byrne's most recent poetry collection *Blood/Sugar*, was published by Arc in 2009. *Bones Will Crow: 15 Contemporary Burmese Poets*, published in June 2012, is co-edited with ko ko thett and is the first anthology of Burmese poetry ever to be published in the West (Arc, 2012 / Northern Illinois University Press, 2013). Byrne is the editor of *The Wolf*, an internationally-renowned poetry magazine, which he co-founded in 2002. He won the Treci Trg poetry festival prize in Serbia and his *Selected Poems: The Vanishing House* was published in Belgrade. Byrne is the co-editor of *Voice Recognition: 21 Poets for the 21st Century*, an anthology of poets under 35, published by Bloodaxe in 2009. He lectures on English Literature and Creative Writing and was the Poet in Residence at Clare Hall, University of Cambridge. His poems have been translated into several languages including Arabic, Burmese and Chinese and he is the International Editor for Arc Publications. His next collection is entitled *White Coins* and will be published in 2014.

Lorna Callery: Writer/artist/performer/educator/co-founder: Monosyllabic + Polka Dot Punks. Interests: concrete/site-specific poetry + all things 'pop-up'.

'Execution of a teenage girl' was written in response to a documentary on TV about the inequality of women in the Middle East. I couldn't stop thinking about the tragedy of Atefah's story, a teenage girl who was sexually assaulted and then subsequently murdered as a result of the shame of the attack. I felt that it was important to tell her story.

Richy Campbell's work has appeared in *Popshot Magazine* and INDENT; he had a poem shortlisted for the 2011 Live Canon Poetry Prize and a chapbook longlisted for the 2013 Venture Award. Richy lives and studies in Manchester.

'Pyongyang City' is a reaction to researching the human rights situation in North Korea and wanting to raise awareness through various depictions of it. Inspired by the nation's capital, the poem tries to reveal that city's ornamental, synthetic nature. The theme of absence, and its eeriness, also runs through the verse. During my research into the topic I watched some documentaries, and read books and articles. Here are the most memorable: Crossing the Line *(documentary);* Aquariums of Pyongyang *by Kang-Chol Hwan;* Nothing to Envy *by Barbara Demick.*

Lorraine Caputo is a documentary poet and activist. Her works appear in over 70 journals in Canada, the US and Latin America, as well as seven chapbooks of poetry, five audio recordings and six anthologies. She went into exile over a decade ago and has been travelling through Latin America since.

'Silent courage' has three parts: I. Chajul and II. San Juan Cotzal, both written during my visit to the Ixil Triangle in March 1994; and III. Santiago Atitlán, from my April 1992 visit to that village. The anthology features the second part of this poem, my documentation from San Juan Cotzal. In all three towns I saw the memorials the people had erected in the churches, despite the fact that the civil war and repression were still occurring full force. I was struck by these people's silent courage. These were two of the areas hardest hit by massacres committed by government forces (both the military and the Patrullas de Autodefensa Civil). It is for the massacres in the Ixil Triangle that retired general Efraím Ríos Montt, military dictator of Guatemala from 1982 to 1983, is currently on trial. In the 1980s, I became involved in Central American solidarity work in the US. I wanted to learn more, to see with my own eyes, hear with my own ears what was happening. Since the late 1980s, I have made several journeys to Guatemala, learning about the history and culture of the pueblos there, and sharing those lessons with others through poetry. Until the Peace Accords were signed in 1996, thus ending Guatemala's 36-year-old Civil War, travelling in that country was an experience. One learned the old adage of travelling in war zones: To keep your eyes and ears well open, and your mouth well-shut. I learned much, behind closed doors and in silent witness, from the Guatemala peoples.

Srinjay Chakravarti is a 40-year-old writer, journalist, researcher and translator based in Salt Lake City, Calcutta, India. He has worked as an editor with an international online financial news service. He was educated at St Xavier's College, Calcutta and at universities in Calcutta and New Delhi (BSc Economics; MA English).

'Free lunch' was inspired by a news report that was published in a Bengali (Bangla) daily newspaper of Kolkata. As the item noted, the people who forage for samples of the rice being sold in Burdwan cannot be considered beggars; they merely prevent these small amounts of food-grains from going to waste and, in that way, get their daily sustenance. They congregate at the Sadar Ghat bus stand before dawn, as otherwise they might miss the trucks and buses that enter Burdwan town with their cargoes of rice every morning; missing even one of these means that much less food on their plates that day.

There is a public distribution system which, however, does not function very well. The federal and state governments are also taking measures to ensure food security for all in India. Yet the starving poor regularly congregate at the bus stand of this town in West Bengal. Partly the result of systemic, endemic corruption and deep-rooted social prejudices, this phenomenon shows how Indians are both cruel and generous, both ruthless and kind at one and the same time. The agricultural middlemen and brokers refuse to distribute free food among the starving, since commercial transactions in food-grains form their livelihood, their vocation. However, they do not begrudge donating them the excess food-grains that gather during the course of their day's work; rather than throw the samples of rice away, they drop these into the palms of the waiting poor. A sort of warped capitalist work ethic. They refuse to let the rice go to waste, which is of course a most noble sentiment —though they agree to give it away only as long as it is in the form of alms, which, again, is a rather perverted form of charity.

Mary Jean Chan was born and raised in Hong Kong, and is currently an MPhil in development studies candidate at the University of Oxford. In March 2012 she gave a TEDx talk entitled: 'A Tapestry of Narratives: Conversations Through Poetry', in which she discussed poetry's role in building a better society through fostering genuine discourse and dialogue.

'The taming': there is a Chinese banyan tree along the roadside where I take my dog every morning during the summer holidays spent at home in Hong Kong. One morning, I passed by that very same tree and noticed (for the first time) how its roots looked eerily like the arteries of a human being. This poem was born out of my thoughts about how the recognition that humanity has always been inseparable from Nature might enable us to begin to take proactive steps towards healing our increasingly plundered and fevered Earth.

Deepak Chaswal is a poet from the soil of India. He is also a professor of English. His poetry exhibits his perception of the universe from the perspective of an insider. Deepak's poems have been published in reputable international poetry journals like *Sam Smith, The Journal, Pacific Review, Pamona Valley Review, Forge, Enchanting Verses, The Tower, Earthborne Poetry Magazine, Kritya – A Journal of Poetry, Indian Ruminations, Bicycle Review, Electronic Monsoon Magazine, Efiction Notice, Frog Croon, Message in a Bottle Poetry Magazine* to name just a few. His poems are often inspired by 21st-century complexities and problems related to the violation of human rights.

Linda Cosgriff is an Open University graduate. She has been published in anthologies, online and has had success in poetry competitions. She was shortlisted for the 2012 *erbacce* poetry prize. Her poetry has been turned into art. Much of her work is inspired by the 14 years she spent living in South Africa, during and after apartheid. This poem was written in tribute to Johannesburg newspaper, *The Star*, which regularly ran blank space in protest at the apartheid regime's censorship. Linda writes a popular humorous blog at http://thelaughinghousewife.wordpress.com.

David J. Costello lives in Wallasey, Merseyside. He co-hosts local poetry venues The Bards (of New Brighton) and Liver Bards and is a member of both Chester Poets and North West Poets. David has been widely published, most recently in *The Penny Dreadful* (Rep. of Ireland), *Envoi, Magma* and *The Passionate Transitory*. He also won the 2011 Welsh Poetry Competition.

'Lord's Resistance Army' was written as a direct response to an interview on BBC 4's Today programme in which a young woman described how the Lord's Resistance Army (in Uganda) were imposing their will on the rural population through a deliberate policy of mutilation, particularly of women. She and her two friends were abducted and appallingly disfigured while carrying water back to their village.

Barbara Cumbers is a geology lecturer and librarian, living in London with her husband and two cats. She has published poems in magazines including *Rialto, Smith's Knoll, Poetry London*, and is currently working on a first collection.

'Thirst fugue' uses the style of a famous poem by Paul Celan, many of whose relatives died in Nazi death camps. I am not drawing parallels with the death camps, but the obvious

similarities between the Israeli treatment of the Palestinians and the pre-war Nazi treatment of the Jews – driving them out of areas wanted for settlements, ghettoisation – justify the use of the poem. I have used water supply as my basis because Palestinian farms are deliberately deprived of water by Israeli settlers.

George Roddam Currie is an emeritus lecturer in education and has studied the Holocaust for over 40 years.

'A potato': I feel weighed down, not only by the heavy burden of the knowledge I possess, but more so by the heavy moral responsibility for this weight of knowledge – in the sense of hoping that it may not happen again if this knowledge is kept safe for future generations. I believe poetry is the way to convey the emotion and feeling of the Holocaust for future generations as it causes one to learn through emotion as well as fact.

John Daniel has had poems widely published in magazines, and is the author of three volumes, the most recent being *Skinning the Bull* by Oversteps.

'Chinese Kidneys' was inspired by an article I read in a newspaper.

I wrote 'EOKA Museum' after visiting it while on holiday in Cyprus.

Claudia Daventry is a travelled poet, writer and teacher, currently living in Scotland to research a PhD on poetry. Her last home was Amsterdam, where she first started to perform her own work: now it's more page than stage. She has won various awards and commendations, including the Bridport Prize in 2012.

'Loud': I travelled extensively through China back in 1987, two years before Tiananmen Square, and was haunted by not only the poverty but the oppression. Deng Xiaoping had introduced the Open Door policy to the West, to boost foreign trade, but the whole of China was still suffering from the impact of the Cultural Revolution and the resulting regression. Above all, amid the naïve optimism of the younger people there was faith – in a regime which had destroyed culture and education and treated individuals with such terrible disrespect – and a genuine belief that, in spite of the illiteracy and devastation, the country was now about to reap the benefits. However, individual freedom was still tightly controlled, down to not speaking too loud on trains and buses, and if individuals dared to breach the rules the punishment could be death. The newspaper sheets pasted on the village walls showed pictures of these 'criminals' with descriptions of their crimes: moving to another province without permission to be with a woman; one man had stolen a bicycle. One day I saw a truckload of bound men being driven away to be shot. The image has never left me. This poem has an anonymous setting with a generic, mid-European feel, because since my experience in China I've travelled in countries closer to home which have suffered similar brutality. While I was living in Amsterdam I was inspired by the work of two courageous women, Dubravka Ugresic and Ayaan Hirsi Ali, both strangers to the Netherlands and both speaking out strongly against the oppressive regimes they had left behind. The truth is, it's everywhere: specific incidents and first-hand accounts really stand for a bigger picture. Western indifference makes us into tourists looking into these lives from the outside.

Tracy Davidson lives in Warwickshire and enjoys writing poetry and flash fiction. Her work has appeared in various publications and anthologies including *Writing Magazine*,

Mslexia, Modern Haiku, Atlas Poetica and *A Hundred Gourds.*

'The forgotten ones' was inspired by reading a BBC online news report about a car bombing in a food market in the Sadriya district of Baghdad which occurred in April 2007. The events in the poem itself are pure fiction, just trying to imagine what the carnage and terror must have been like.

Miriam Davies is from Sussex and recently completed a creative writing course at the University of Brighton.

'The wall': while volunteering in the West Bank in 2005 I saw an elderly Palestinian lady with heavy shopping bags being turned away from a checkpoint in the Israeli barrier near the town of Bethany. She then had to struggle up a steep hill towards the next checkpoint to try again so that she could get home. This for me brought to life the everyday effects on the civilian population of restrictions on freedom of movement.

Deepa Dharmadhikari grew up in Delhi, and has returned to live and work there after a five-year stint of educational self-exile abroad.

'The Indian woman' came about after encountering one too many comments from people in the West that made assumptions about Indian women based on a history of racism, Orientalism and exoticism.

Brian Docherty was born in Glasgow, lives in north London, and was educated at Middlesex Polytechnic, University of Essex, University of London Institute of Education and St Mary's University College Twickenham. His three books are *Armchair Theatre* (Hearing Eye), *Desk with a View* (Hearing Eye) and *Woke up this Morning* (Smokestack Books).

'Junk mail' was written after watching a report on BBC London news featuring a teenage boy who had grown up in south London, but came originally from Somalia (or possibly Ethiopia) as a small child. He looked, talked and walked like any other south London kid, regarded the city as his home, attended a London school, and may not have had any surviving family in his ancestral homeland, but was about to be deported to a country he did not remember because of some anomaly in his status or paperwork.

Cath Drake is an Australian from Perth. Lured to London in 2001, she has been published in anthologies and magazines in UK, Australia and the US. She has performed her work in cafes, bookshops, theatres, festivals, at Southbank, Tate Modern, and for unsuspecting passers-by. She has an interest in taking poetry and creative writing to new spaces and last year as writer-in-residence at the Albany Arts Centre cafe she created activities that included community books and impromptu performances. She was awarded an Arts Council England grant and was shortlisted for the Venture poetry award in 2012. Also a non-fiction writer, her work includes award-winning journalism, writing for radio, oral history and life stories. See http://cathdrake.com.

'Finding Australia' is dedicated to my ground-breaking year nine social studies teacher at Hollywood High School in Western Australia. It was a revelation at 14 years old to finally be told the truth about Aboriginal people, see real modern and hear the history of massacres that took place. What I couldn't quite believe was how for me this major part of Australia (past

and present) had been totally left out until then, both in my formal education and anywhere else! There was the odd cartoon-like Aboriginal-with-spear drawing in our project books, and that's all I had known. It made me angry and is one of the biggest lessons I've ever learnt about questioning versions of history. The quatrains hint at a ballad (the typical form of 'bush' poetry).

'Greenies': I worked on environmental issues for a decade. I got so tired of being labelled: many people assumed that if you say you want a healthy environment for everyone then you're a greenie – someone with an extreme agenda. But a healthy environment for all seems like such a reasonable ask!

Carol Ann Duffy is a poet and playwright. She is professor of contemporary poetry at Manchester Metropolitan University, and was appointed Britain's poet laureate in May 2009.

Ann Egan's poetry collections are *Landing the Sea* (Bradshaw Books), *The Wren Women* (Black Mountain Press), *Brigit of Kildare* (Kildare Library and Arts Services and her latest from 2012 is *Telling Time* (Bradshaw Books). She has edited more than 20 books including *The Midlands Arts and Culture Review, 2010*.

'Background' was inspired by the nature all around me near the village of Clane in Ireland. But it exists on a dual level and speaks of a larger world out there.

Ken Evans works in education and lives in the Peak District. Since attending an Arvon Writing course last year, he has written, read and been published at regional poetry events and in magazines.

'Banned UK search terms' is anti-censorship and asks the question 'What if we had banned internet search terms in the UK?' as in China and elsewhere. What might those words include?

'Citizenship test' is a satirical bite at the politicians, law-makers, media and those who govern who think notions of 'Englishness' can be tied down to a prescriptive set of banal, pre-requisite 'knowledges' or series of memory tests – and the idea that this is even in any way desirable.

Kit Fan's first book of poems *Paper Scissors Stone* won the inaugural International HKU Poetry Prize in 2011. His poems have appeared widely in UK poetry magazines including *Poetry Review, Poetry London* and *Poetry Wales.*

Born in Hong Kong, I was ten years old when the Tiananmen Incident happened on 4 June 1989. I remember it was a very hot summer, while I was sitting in the breathlessly stuffy classroom doing what seemed endless examinations. In the background were the images of students, protestors, tents, tanks broadcasted on HK TV channels which my classmates too would have seen. But the classroom was dead quiet. In fact the whole school was dead quiet during the examination season.

In early July after the exams, the school organised a memorial day and gathered all teachers and students in the assembly hall. There were at least one thousand students in the hall, with fans spinning overhead, before the luxury of air conditioning. We sang together for hours on end – songs of nationalism and mourning, loss and grief, rivers, mountains and the land. I was too young to understand what was going on. Singing was what we all did, and singing, it seemed, was what we all needed to do.

In summer 2012 I returned to Hong Kong for a visit. Liu Xiaobo's June Fourth Elegies had just been published in spring. As I packed my bags, I took the book out, fearing what implications it might bring as I travelled through Mainland China. I was self-censoring. I returned to the primary school for a visit, the first time since I'd left. It was mid July. The examination was over. The school was deserted but the poem arrived in the rain.

Mark Fiddes is a former finalist in the National Poetry Competition and has just been Highly Commended in the Gregory O'Donoghue Prize. His fiction has also been published in last year's *Fish Publishing Anthology* and the *Lightship Anthology* (Alma Books).

The inspiration for the poem 'Before we crossed to Timbuktu' comes from a trip a few years ago to the Tuareg music festival in Essakane, Mali. Many of the kids we met along the way were working in hard labour with no prospect of education. The pencils we gave out were treated as toys ... although the incident related in the poem really happened. Seeing the brutal invasion this year with Ansar Dine – who were burning precious books in the nearby ancient library of Timbuktu – made me realise that education is not only the casualty of poverty but also of intolerance and violence.

Robert Fieldhouse has written human rights and social justice poems for many years. He went to Goldsmiths College in 1970 and became a graduate and English teacher. Later, he worked as a lecturer in a local college for 20 years, educating adults with learning difficulties and mental health problems. These people were kicked out of college, so he resigned. Human rights had been expelled and other social services will have to pay more money to deal with them. He has also written a children's story based on human rights. It will become an ebook soon.

The poem is not inspired by any particular event, but rather is a short look at sweatshop labour, the idea of seasons across farming and fashion, and the appropriation of language. 'Plum rain' (Meiyu in Chinese) is a colloquial term for the fat rains of the Asian rainy season, essential for farming cycles.

Camila Fiori is a performer and cross-disciplinary artist. Her work takes several forms, playing in the spaces between ... boundaries ... cultures ... languages ... 'audience'/'performer' ... the (un)/(mis)spoken word. Having grown up between London and Rio, in a home where five languages interchanged frequently and a sentence constructed in just one tongue was rare, much of her work explores language crossover and (mis)translation/understanding. London's rich cultural diversity and the layers of migration throughout her family hugely inform the themes she is so often drawn back to.

'Swollen' is born from a lifelong fear of, and fascination with, the place and sound of silence: that which is left unsaid – through selection, censorship or fragmented memory. It is the dialogue between the spoken and unspoken, the paradox of potential power they both carry, that's at the heart of the piece. As part of a multi-layered project dealing with the repercussions of the brutal dictatorship in Chile (from which my parents fled in 1973), it is intrinsically linked to long-swallowed words and incomplete pictures – both my own and those of others. In

many parts of the world that have endured violent regimes, particularly in Latin America, there has been an unacknowledged culture of 'forgetting'. This is poisonous. Not speaking of, somehow containing the torment of the past, can become a way of defining 'democracy', moving on, maintaining peace. But the wounds, though covered over, cannot be healed, fostering the potential for re-occurrence. I hope to question this shroud of silence, while stimulating thought, humanity, and perhaps inspiring change.

Kate Firth is a poet living in Bristol. She also works as a voice therapist, helping others find their voice, and as a consultant to The Alliance for Religions and Conservation on *Values Quest*, a joint project with the Club of Rome.

'The laughing farmers' was inspired by a very short article I read years ago in the New Internationalist about 50,000 Indian farmers in Karnataka attempting to 'laugh out' a corrupt official in their attempt to bring about land reform and an increase in the price of their produce. I finally googled for more information last year, and found a longer article, 'Out of India: grin mightier than the sword (The Independent, 26 September 1992), telling the story of Mr Nanjunda Swamy, a law professor from Bangalore who, inspired by Gandhi's non-violent approach, organised the challenge to 'the state's despotic Chief Minister, S. Bangarappa, by laughing at him in a big way'. Apparently the government had refused to listen to their requests and protesters had either been 'arrested or shot.' Mr Swamy organised the 50,000 by initially telling jokes about Mr Bangarappa to warm them up and very soon just the mention of the name 'Bangarappa' made everybody howl with laughter. The police made no arrests and although Mr Bangarappa couldn't be shamed into resigning, his reputation among the 'laughing farmers,' as I call them, was shattered.

Vee Freir is a semi-retired clinical psychologist living in the Scottish Borders, who has been writing poetry for the last five years. She has had poems published in *The Eildon Tree* (the literary magazine from the Scottish Borders Council) issues 21 and 22, as well as in the Borders Writers Forum Anthologies of 2011 and 2012.

'Kora in Lhasa': apart from loving Scotland, I have an interest in Buddhism and one of my pleasures is to visit countries which have a Buddhist heritage. In 2006 I was lucky enough to go to teachings with His Holiness The Dalai Lama and was most struck by his words, 'You must go and visit Tibet, but go with open eyes.' So I did. I went across country from Kathmandu, Nepal to Lhasa in Tibet in October 2006, wrote a daily journal of my travels and the many things I saw, and have been writing poems and stories from that journal ever since. I witnessed many instances of Tibetan subjugation at the hands of the Chinese authorities, one of which was the daily Kora – the traditional circumambulation – Tibetan people performed around the Potala Palace, which touched my heart. The Chinese army (and therefore the authorities) would only let the Tibetans do the Kora in certain places, in spite of the fact that the Potala Palace is a Tibetan spiritual 'home' and part of their rich culture. The Potala and the freedom to practice their spirituality around it should be open and available for Tibetans as, after all, our spirituality is our human right.

Gwen Garnier-Duguy's poetry was first published in 1995 in the surrealist-inspired review *Supérieur Inconnu* and continued to appear in the publication until 2005. In 2003 he participated in a colloquium on the poet Patrice de la Tour du Pin at the Collège de

France and gave a presentation on the poetics of absence central to La Quête de Joie. Fascinated by the painting of Robert Mangú, Garnier-Duguy wrote a novel on the artist, Nox, published by the Éditions le Grand Souffle. His poems have also been published in the reviews *Sarrazine, La Soeur de l'Ange, POESIEDirecte, Les cahiers du sens, Le Bateau Fantôme, La main millénaire, Nunc, Les hommes sans épaules*, Phoenix, Siècle 21, *Ditch poetry* (Canada), *Polja* (Serbie) and *The Enchanting Verses Literary Review* (Inde). His poem 'Sainteté je marche vers toi' was published in *L'année poétique*, 2009, by Seghers. In 2011 Éditions de l'Atlantique published his first collection of poetry *Danse sur le territoire, amorce de la parole*, with a preface by Michel Host, recipient of the Goncourt prize in 1986. Gwen Garnier-Duguy and Matthieu Baumier founded the online magazine *Recours au poème* (www.recoursaupoème.com) devoted to international poetry in May 2012.

Steve Garside is a poet, painter and photographer from Rochdale, Lancashire. He has been published in the US and UK and has exhibited his work in the UK and EU. He lives in Manchester.

Inspiration for 'Tidal flow': I went to the Hay Festival in 2012 and listened to and later met with the Syrian poet and activist Faraj Bayrakdar. I wrote this poem in response to how I felt inspired by him, his poetry and humility.

John Gibbens was born in Cheshire in 1959 and grew up in West Germany and west Cumbria. He moved to London at 18, where he has worked as typist, secretary, typesetter and, latterly, a Fleet Street subeditor. His poetry won an Eric Gregory Award in 1982. He self-published *Collected Poems* in 2000 and *The Nightingale's Code: a poetic study of Bob Dylan* in 2001. His first book with a publishing house, *Orpheus Ascending*, appeared from Smokestack Books in 2012.

No particular incident inspired 'Mother & child', but a lifetime of hearing reports of bloodshed from the region where so much of our way of life – our agriculture, our cities, our mathematics, our religion – first arose. I was prompted to submit it, however, by the coverage today, 15 May 2013, of Conscientious Objectors Day; and by learning that in modern Israel – whose ancient namesake bequeathed us the phrase 'Thou shalt not kill' – there is no legal recognition of conscientious objection. This anomaly is currently highlighted by the case of 19-year-old Natan Blanc, who has just received a tenth prison sentence for his refusal to serve in the Israeli Defence Forces.

Laurice Gilbert is President of the New Zealand Poetry Society, with poems published in many New Zealand journals and anthologies, *Island* (Australia), *The Book of Ten* (UK), *Shot Glass Journal, Fib Review* and *Sugar Mule* (online). She is the current Featured Poet International at Muse-Pie Press, and published her first collection, *My Family & Other Strangers*, in December 2012. She recently won second prize in the 2013 Caselberg International Poetry Competition, and her current project is a joint collection with Portuguese poet Hugo Kauri Justo.

'Jason' was inspired by a photograph and story in an Oxfam newsletter. I was impressed by the child's determination to make the most of the education offered him in unpromising conditions.

Chrissie Gittins's poetry collections are *Armature* (Arc) and *I'll Dress One Night as You* (Salt). She has made a recording for the Poetry Archive and has read at the Hay, Edinburgh, Aldeburgh and Ledbury festivals and at the Poets House New York. Chrissie is Lewisham's first honorary writer-in-residence.

'No further': I hired a tour guide in Mae Hong Son, the most northerly province in Thailand. He skewed the itinerary so that we visited a camp of 2,000 Karenni refugees from Burma. The tour guide was himself a Karenni.

'Frontiers': I remembered a story that a Karenni politician in exile had told me when I was about to board a plane at Gatwick.

Sue Guiney is a poet and novelist living in London. She is a writer-in-residence in the Southeast Asian Department of the University of London's School of Oriental and African Studies (SOAS); and also runs a writing workshop for street kids in Siem Reap, Cambodia.

'Mekong women': three years of working in Cambodia have given me a clear view of the difficult role of women in that precarious and developing country. Women are often belittled and ignored, even though much of the work is done by them. Women often find themselves cast out of their homes because of illnesses brought back to them by their husbands. There is also a problem of poverty which can lead families to sell their daughters into the sex trade. Yet Khmer women are powerful and strong and they are now beginning to find ways to give voice to that strength. A recent example is the women-only demonstration in the streets of Phnom Penh against forced evictions. While researching women's health issues for my new novel, Out of the Ruins, *I became more sensitive to the difficult lives of women in modern day Cambodia. This poem grew out of that research, which led to conversations with women on the streets of Phnom Penh and observations of brothels in the back roads of Siem Reap. Ultimately, I was inspired by their refusal to buckle under the weight of their alienation, and their undiminished sense of pride.*

'Speech found': about a year ago, a group of writers, entertainers and scholars went to Parliament to deliver a petition in favour of libel reform. I was one of the poets to sit in on the parliamentary discussion and then carry the petition to Downing Street. I wrote the first draft of this poem as a result of that experience. In April of this year, the new law surrounding libel reform again came under fire and I found myself revisiting and revising this poem. As a writer living in Britain, I liked to think I was immune to the sorts of censorship I have witnessed during my work in Southeast Asia. But freedom of speech is a very tenuous freedom and one which is easily lost. The fact that we could so easily lose it here in Britain calls for action, including poetry.

Alyson Hallett lives in Falmouth and is currently going through the proofs of her second book of poems. She runs an international poetry as public art project, The Migration Habits of Stones, works part-time as a fellow with the Royal Literary Fund and swims in the sea whenever she can. For more information please visit www.thestonelibrary.com

I was living in Hartland, a small village in North Devon, when I wrote 'To the men of Guantanamo Bay'. I loved living in the village – I felt very safe there and would even go walking

on my own late at night in the woods. When I heard about the suicides in Guantanamo I didn't know what to do. I was beside myself to think that I was safe and happy while others were wracked with fear. I remembered Neruda's poem, and how every poet is obliged to take the freedom they feel and share it with those who are not so lucky.

Maggie Harris is a Guyana-born writer living in the UK. She writes both poetry and prose.

Inspiration for 'For an Afghan woman poet' came from an article in The Sunday Times *some years ago which told the story of a woman poet called Nadia from Afghanistan and her struggle to have the freedom to write. She was part of a 'sewing club' where women came together to write under the cover of needlework. She was forced into marriage and subsequently murdered by her husband, who was not punished for his crime. I used the magazine article to raise awareness in my women's writing group and inspire a response from them. This poem came out of that.*

Benjamin Hayes is a psychology graduate, stats geek, and part-time poet from Shropshire. He now calls London home.

'Marriage equality' was inspired by disillusionment with the attitudes of fellow straight people, religious leaders and government officials who feel that they are entitled to a controlling opinion on a human rights issue that bears no consequence to their own lives. But I guess that's our democracy at work.

Jasmine Heydari is an MA creative writing student at Kingston University in London. She was born in Iran during the Iran–Iraq war and later emigrated to Sweden at the age of six with her mother and sister. After graduating from university, she moved to Beijing to study Mandarin and work as a translator. Writing is her passion and eternal love. She published her first poem collection in Sweden at the age of 17 and in 2012 published a short story in an anthology of Swedish writers. She is currently working on her first novel in English, about friendship and intercultural relationships set in contemporary China.

'32-inch flat screen TV set' is my first poem describing the events during and after a war. I think it is important to realise that when a war finishes, it never really ends for those who have survived it, that something always triggers memories of the conflict no matter how hard we try to escape from them. I hope by reading this poem and sharing my own personal experiences, people will understand the depth of war and the scars that never fully heal, no matter how hard we try.

Yewa Holiday is a full-time PhD candidate at Queen Mary, University of London where she has been awarded a graduate teaching assistantship. Her research is on the prosecution of asylum seekers and refugees for offences relating to entry to or presence in England, Wales and Northern Ireland without any – or insufficient – regard to Article 31 of the 1951 Refugee Convention. She was called to the Bar at Middle Temple in 1996. She has LLMs in International Law (Cambridge, First class) and International Criminal Law (Sussex, Distinction). Yewa also works part-time at the Criminal Cases Review Commission. She writes poetry and short stories.

'The Christmas my mother wrote Samwise Gamgee': the human rights situation is implied rather than directly described in this poem, loosely based on what happened in Sierra Leone in 1967–8. In this period, three coups took place after the African People's Congress won its first election, having beaten the incumbent Sierra Leonean Peoples Party. I was born in Bo and my family lived in Kenema. The poem is told from my perspective as a small child 'remembering' fragments of my life in the shadow of the presence of soldiers and a mother who refused to take them seriously. It seemed that even the environment reflected the tenseness of a political situation which had been developing prior to 1967. At the edge of our lives hovered the threat of death in the form of devil dances which terrified me as a child. My mother's car, Samwise Gamgee, was a reliable constant to the changing political backdrop. The 'dried blood' of the lettering on my mother's car is a forewarning of danger, not only in relation to the three coups between 1967–8 but also to subsequent coups and the ten-year civil war which ended in 2002.

Isha lives in the UK.

'Request for assistance' is about my attempts to get appropriate medical help for my physical condition. It seemed to me that my doctors were ignoring my requests for help because someone had decided that I was a mental health case, and when I did eventually receive assistance for my mental health (after a total breakdown caused by several years of appalling pain and lack of sleep), I was treated inhumanely by a psychiatrist in front of a roomful of people, none of whom intervened. And still I didn't get help for my physical condition, which wasn't diagnosed until many years later. Also, no-one offered help or spoke to me when I was creeping along the pavement banging my head against the walls of buildings because of the level of pain I was suffering. These are only two examples of the way I was badly treated as a vulnerable person in a very bad physical condition. All the above experiences were at the hands of the National Health Service.

Nabila Jameel is a British Pakistani poet, working and living in Manchester. Her poems have been published by *Stand* magazine, the *Poetry Review* and in a recent anthology by Bloodaxe, *Out of Bounds*. She taught English in the further education sector and now works for a publisher. She has also recently contributed a chapter to an academic book discussing the importance of performance for all writers and is currently working on her first poetry collection, which is a series of critical snapshots of society.

Keith Jarrett lives and works in London. A former London and UK poetry slam champion, he teaches spoken word in secondary schools and is working on his first novel.

'Asylum cocktails' was inspired by the words of Judge Lord Rodger on the HJ and HT v. Home Secretary (2010) ruling allowing LGBT people the right to apply for asylum in the UK on the basis of their sexuality and fear of persecution: 'What is protected is the applicant's right to live freely and openly as a gay man. To illustrate the point with trivial stereotypical examples from British society: just as male heterosexuals are free to enjoy themselves playing rugby, drinking beer and talking about girls with their mates, so male homosexuals are to be free to enjoy themselves going to Kylie concerts, drinking exotically coloured cocktails and talking about boys with their straight female mates.'

Richard Tyrone Jones is the director of 'Utter!', the spoken word at Edinburgh's Free Fringe and creator of a 'fascinating, sobering, hilarious, and ultimately uplifting' (says the *New Scientist*) five-star solo show and BBC radio 4 mini-series 'Richard Tyrone Jones's Big Heart'. His imagistic, ironic but compassionate work has appeared in *Magma, Rising, Delinquent, South Bank Poetry, Morning Star,* and his books *Germline* and *Big Heart* are 'often witty, sometimes unsettling and always smart' – Tim Key.

With 'Parsing' I wanted to pay tribute to the bravery and obstinacy of writers progressively oppressed, silenced and murdered, in a way parsed down to their most important elements, by fascists, communists (Lorca, Kharms) and religious fundamentalists (Warsame Shire Awale, murdered in Somalia, 2012). The pen is not always as mighty as the sword, but the spirit of art, of resistance, is irrepressible. www.bbc.co.uk/news/world-africa-20135824.

'We need a victim' is a more blackly ironic piece about child abuse and how the media's need for a story can compromise the human rights of victims. These victims, as in the Savile case, often only get the choice of whether or not to bear witness following their abusers' deaths. This could be many years after the initial abuse – and then only if the media finds their story interesting or credible enough. That is when their second ordeal – the modern show trial – begins.

Esther Kamkar was born and raised in Tehran, Iran. Her poetry book *Hum of Bees* was published in 2011. She lives and works in Palo Alto, California.

'No school for children in a time of war' was inspired by the work of the Syrian poet Adonis. When I hear and read about any human rights violations in the world, I start reading the literature, the poetry of that region.

Kayleigh Kavanagh is a graduate of the University of Cumbria. As a writer she experiments with various mediums, repeatedly creating new and engaging material. She interned for a writing development agency and publishers, and learnt extensively from this experience. To date she has published several poems, a play and a playella.

'Vegetable': I suffer from ME/CFS so am well aware how it feels to be trapped in your own body and the prejudices that surround disabled persons such as myself. Also when I was well, I interned for Commonword, and was project manager for an event on abuse and the hidden victims of the UK – focusing largely on the sex trade and the asylum seekers – which also influenced my work.

Alia' Afif Kawalit is a postgraduate research student under the supervision of Professor Janet Montefiore. Some of her poems have been published in *Route 57* and *Best of Manchester Poets Vol. 2*. She was featured in Manchester's Not Part of Festival, Grey Area Gallery and Margate's Turner Gallery and co-organised and took part in the literary symposium Hospitality Poetica at Notre Dame University. In addition, she participates in poetry readings around the UK.

'Turning a blind eye' is inspired by the relationship between the media and human rights. The challenge is not only in protecting the rights of journalists but also in providing the readers and the audience with transparent and unbiased information.

Shamshad Khan's poetry collection *Megalomaniac* is published by Salt Publishing (2007). She has been commissioned to write for BBC Radio 3 and the Manchester Museum. Her performances have included collaborations with beat boxers and musicians. She has experience of running creative writing workshops for survivors of domestic violence, men and women in prisons, Asian women, academics and young people. Her current writing explores themes of love and spiritual longing.

I was commissioned and inspired to write 'Angel on the right' in response to 'Safe to Return? – Pakistani women, domestic violence and access to refugee protection – A report of a transnational research project conducted in the UK and Pakistan' by South Manchester Law Centre and Manchester Metropolitan University. The poem refers to how religion, and in this case Islam, can be used as a means to protect women. It recounts how at the time of the prophet Mohammed women had significant and powerful public roles and actively participated in society. Inspiration was taken from oft-quoted sayings from religious texts. The two angels (Raqib and Atid) reputed to record our good and bad deeds are acknowledged. The poem suggests a subtle defiance as the woman prays whilst blood drips down her thighs. It is often interpreted that Islam prohibits women from performing prayer during menstruation. There is intentional ambiguity in the poem as the source of the blood may be the result of the violence perpetrated against the woman. The subtext is that God can only be a loving God, not one who endorses violence or coercion of any kind. The poem draws on and celebrates women's achievements, ingenuity and defiance in the face of oppression.

'None's hands' was written as part of a commission in response to the report referred to above ('Safe to Return?'). The report looked at the impact of legislation on instances of domestic violence, in particular how the rules around 'leave to remain', 'the two year rule' and 'no recourse to public funds' make it more difficult for women to leave abusive relationships. The main inspiration for the poem is the resilience of women survivors who are brave enough to report cases of domestic violence, despite all the pressures against them. The report included personal accounts from women who were often not believed or understood and of the pressures they were under to prove their experiences to the statutory bodies. It also highlighted the lack of cultural and emotional awareness and the need for more sensitive and robust laws to protect women. The poem 'None's hands' challenges us to think how we may all be implicated in the perpetuation of injustice, even if only by our inaction.

Jasmine King was born in the south-west of England and has lived in London for the last 20 years. She currently works in the voluntary sector in the East End.

'That's one of them' was inspired by those occasions when I have felt fear towards those who seemed different or alien to me. Unfortunately this is a common human reaction.

Anthony Levin is a writer, teacher and human rights lawyer who has worked for ten years with refugees, prisoners and survivors of torture. As a writer, he has published poetry and prose, and written for magazines such as *Men's Style*, *Prospect Magazine* and News Limited. As an early-career academic, his research includes the intersection between literature and human rights, and post-Holocaust fiction. He is Vice-President of the Australian Association of Jewish Holocaust Survivors & Descendants, and a Director of Attorneys for the Rights of the Child.

'Blood moon' was written in response to events that took place during the Civil War in Syria. In June 2011, the Syrian government led an assault on Homs, identified as the 'capital' of the resistance, as well as other cities. Violence has continued since that time, with evidence of recent massacres and crimes against humanity in cities such as Houla and Latakia. Coincidentally, there was a total lunar eclipse on 15 June 2011, during which the moon had a reddish hue.

Liang Yujing writes in both English and Chinese. Publications include *Wasafiri, Weyfarers, Acumen, Litro, Boston Review, Westerly* and many others. He is a lecturer at Hunan University of Commerce, China.

Pippa Little is Scottish but grew up in Tanzania. Her poetry collection *Overwintering* came out from Oxford Poets/Carcanet Press in October 2012.

'Poem for Nasrin': Nasrin Sotoudeh is a human rights lawyer in Iran. She has represented opposition activists and highlighted the executions of children. She was jailed in September 2010 for 11 years and went on a 49-day hunger strike until December 2012 when the authorities lifted the travel restrictions they had imposed on her daughter. She was a winner of the European Parliament's Sakharov Prize for Freedom of Thought in 2012. Nasrin can be supported through Amnesty International.

Nasrin Sotoudeh is a hugely courageous and principled woman who has sacrificed her own life and relationships with family and friends as well as her distinguished legal career in order to stand up against injustice and an oppressive state. Since learning of her from Amnesty International and discovering how many people and groups all over the world support her, I have tried my best to help too. That's why I wrote this poem.

Bárbara L. López Cardona was born in Medellín, Colombia. She moved to London in the 80's and studied Creative Writing, Theatre and English. She has been writing poetry since an early age and short stories recently. Some of her work has been published in the Spanish anthology of short stories and poetry - Fantasmas, Amor y Mas - as well as in various Latin-American online cultural magazines.

The armed conflict in Colombia, where kidnapping, rape and killings have been the order of the day for more than 50 years, inspired me to write this poem about the emotional traumas that such events leave on their victims.

Eamonn Lynskey is a Dublin poet. His work first appeared in the *New Irish Writing* pages of the *Irish press*, edited by David Marcus and since then widely in magazines and journals such as *Poetry Ireland Review, Cyphers, The Shop, Crannog, Revival, The Stony Thursday Book* and *The Stinging Fly.* He was a finalist in the Strokestown International Poetry Competition (2004) and in the Sunday Tribune Hennessy Awards (2005). He has published two collections, *Dispatches & Recollections* (Lapwing, Belfast, 1998) and *And Suddenly the Sun Again* (Seven Towers, Dublin, 2010). Eamonn has read and performed his work in Dublin and other Irish cities and in London.

The inspiration for 'Civilian executions, Minsk 1941' is a photograph in the book which accompanies the TV programme 'The Nazis: A Warning from History'. This photograph has haunted me ever since I first saw it and makes me ask the age-old question once again: how can we do this to each other? And I come to the age-old conclusion that the hard work of setting out the parameters of human rights must continue and, as far as possible, be enforced. Particularly pathetic in the photograph is the way the woman must forever remain unnamed and unknown – as were (and are) by far the vast majority of those men, women and children whose human rights are abused.

Kathryn Lund was the winner of the 2012 Grace Dieu Short Story Competition and its 2013 judge. Her story is online at www.gracedieuwriterscircle.co.uk. Two of her poems are being published by Thynks Publishers in *Healing Poems* and *Christmas Poems* (2012 Christmas second-place winner, also online at www.thynkspublications.wordpress.com/prize-winning-poems/).

'A lesson with children': about a month ago Channel 4 News ran a series of documentaries about the conflict in Syria. One of these focused on the plight of children caught in the fighting and featured two boys working at a hospital. One of these boys died as a result of the violence in the region. It reminded me of a conversation I'd had with my niece and nephew not long before when I had used the plight of Syrian refugees to try and arbitrate between them when they had been arguing over a toy. This had developed into a wider conversation about children in trouble around the world. My niece and nephew's reaction to this at the time really moved me. I wanted to write this to encapsulate the conversation we had and their response as well as the issue behind it which had inspired the conversation.

PD Lyons's work has appeared in many magazines and e-zines throughout the world. Originally from the USA, PD Lyons has spent much of the last 20 years living and travelling abroad, and is currently residing in Ireland. Two collections of poetry, *Searches for Magic* and *Caribu & Sister Stones*, have been published by Lapwing Press Belfast. Other titles are available via Amazon, Kindle, Create Space and Lu-Lu. For more information and updates please visit http://pdlyons.wordpress.com.

'The orphan as adult' was written upon seeing the famous National Geographic *cover photo of the grown-up Afghan girl who was herself originally on the cover as a child during the Russian involvement in Afghanistan. Twenty years later not much has changed.*

Nick Makoha was born in Uganda and fled the country with his mother, as a result of political overtones that arose from the civil war during the Idi Amin dictatorship. He has lived in Kenya, Saudi Arabia and currently resides in London. Nick has presented his work at many international events and toured for the British Council in Finland, Czech Republic, the US and the Netherlands. His pamphlet, *The Lost Collection of an Invisible Man*, was published by Flipped Eye in 2005 and he has been widely published in journals and anthologies. Recently he completed a project with Tate Modern in which his poem 'Vista' was used as part of a video installation to promote the Turner prize in 2008 for Tate Remix. His poem 'Beatitude' is the newest addition to *Being Human*, the third book in the *Staying Alive* poetry trilogy. *Staying Alive* and its sequel *Being Alive* has introduced many thousands of new readers to contemporary poetry. Nick's poem 'For the king' was shortlisted for the Coffee House Poetry Fourth Troubadour International Poetry Prize and his poem 'Stone' has been shortlisted for the 2010 Arvon International Poetry competition. As a former writer-in-residence for Newham Libraries, he wrote the poem 'Promise to my unborn son' which was published in the anthology *Out Of Bounds* (Bloodaxe, 2012).

'A crocodile eats the sun' and 'A View from Kidepo Valley': my exodus from Uganda because of the Idi Amin regime makes me a product of interculturalism. It means two worlds are ever present in my head – the world I left (Uganda) and the world that knows me. Uganda is always associated with the shadow of Idi Amin. As a writer born in Uganda, I feel I have an obligation to voice the other side of the story. This is my small contribution to the voice of human rights.

Joe Massingham was born in UK but has lived about half his life in Australia. Retired early because of heart problems, he now waits to see medical practitioners, writes and smells the roses. He has lived in Canberra for the past 12 years. Joe has had work published in Australia, Canada, New Zealand, UK, Eire, USA and India.

'Under the Constitution' was written following the recent school massacre in New England and has been brought back to mind following the latest abortive attempt to amend American gun laws. I simply cannot see how any nation can be regarded as civilised while allowing a constitutional right to possess lethal weapons.

Jaki McCarrick is a graduate of Trinity College, Dublin and an award-winning playwright. Her poetry and short stories have appeared in numerous literary journals, including *The Dublin Review, The Warwick Review, Ambit* and *Poetry Ireland Review*. Jaki's debut collection of short fiction, *The Scattering*, was published by Seren Books in March 2013 and is currently Inpress Book of the Month. She was writer-in-residence at the Centre Culturel Irlandais in Paris from April to June 2013 and is currently finalising her first novel.

'Guernica!' was the headline of a Barcelona newspaper the day after the Madrid bombing of 2004. I was in Barcelona the night before the dead were to be buried – amid vociferous anti-war protests.

Hollie McNish is a UK poet and spoken word artist who Benjamin Zephaniah 'can't take his ears off'. She has released two poetry albums, *Touch* and *Push Kick*, and a first collection of written poetry, *Papers*, in 2012. She runs a poetry organisation, Page to Performance.

'Embarrassed': When Nestlé were scrutinised for human rights abuses in the breastmilk/formula milk scandals, I followed the stories extremely closely and was overwhelmed that companies would target mothers and babies in that way. It was sick. Offering free milk until the mothers' milk dried up and they were then dependent on paying for formula. I remember thinking then how lucky I was to be in the UK, where it didn't happen; where we had an open, unbiased choice between the two. Then when I had a baby, I couldn't believe the amount of pressure there was from advertising, companies and social stigma in general not to breastfeed – including a sales rep being allowed into the hospital ward to give me a 'Bounty Pack' when even my parents weren't allowed in for health and safety reasons.

For someone quite confident in general, I found it so hard to breastfeed in public – especially when I was alone with my child. From comments people made, to the looks I got given (sometimes real sometimes probably imagined), to general insecurities about being a mother. I realized more and more how little we see breastfeeding in soaps, on TV, dramas, adverts etc. It made me really angry that this lack of seeing it was the reason I felt so awkward.

I ended up going into public toilets a lot to feed my daughter. The last time I did so I was reading about the breastmilk scandals which was the motivation for me not to do so again. There is a human right that you can feed a child anywhere but culture and society and business – in the UK and elsewhere – has a role to play in making sure these rights are translated into people actually feeling they can use this right.

Stephen Mead is a published artist, writer, maker of short collage-films and poetry/music mp3s. Much can be learned of his multi-media work by placing his name in any search engine. His latest project-in-progress, a collaborative effort with composer Kevin MacLeod, is entitled 'Whispers of Arias', a two-volume download of narrative poems sung to music. Stephen's latest Amazon release, 'Weightless', a poetry-art hybrid, is a meditation on mortality and perseverance. He lives in New York.

'Power' was influenced by the shock treatment used when homosexuality was still considered a mental illness. Given the fact that reparative therapy still exists, and places where those who are LGBT still face Draconian laws (Uganda, Nigeria, Iran, Iraq etc, etc.), I feel that 'Power' has an imperative to bear witness. I suppose it was also influenced by the work of not only Amnesty International, but such organisations as Truth Wins Out and the work of Peter Tatchell, who was part of the inspiration for my short 2007 YouTube film 'Mercy, Mercy, Mercy', and an essay I wrote later on, 'Am I screaming and do not know it?', about international LGBT persecution.

Joan Michelson, formerly a senior lecturer in English at the University of Wolverhampton, developed and taught both creative writing and Holocaust studies. Publications include 'Irena Klepfisz: Poet-Activist', *Holocaust Literature* (Routledge, 2004) and a collection of Joan's own poetry, *Toward the Heliopause* (Poetic Matrix Publishers, 2011). Her poem 'Muslim Girl' won the 2012 Hamish Canham Prize from the Poetry Society of England. Fiction and essays have been selected for the British Council's volumes, *New Writing*, nos. 3, 4, 14.

'Roll call' draws on The Auschwitz Kommandant: A Daughter's Search for the Father She Never Knew, *a memoir by the German-born American, Barbara Cherish. While sympathetic to her personal trauma, separation, adoption in a foreign land, and growing up forbidden to talk about her blood father without knowing why, I was more than troubled by her blinkered view. She sees her father as a kind, loving victim subject to Berlin. Like the son of Horst von Wächter, whose story was featured in the 3 May 2013 issue of the Financial Times, Barbara Cherish sees her father as 'the good Nazi'. Her filial loyalty overrides and contests the violation of human rights, the legal decision of the International Military Tribunal (1947) and our moral condemnation. Through the mini-narrative portrait of a woman loosely drawn from Barbara Cherish, my intent is to alert us to opposing and slippery thinking around issues of responsibility and judgement. In the fusion of personal and public, the contradictory gains emotional force. Transforming life into art both cools it and mediates between the legacy of trauma and an invitation to reflect upon human, social, ethical and political positions. This prompts us to consider the consequences of our actions and attitudes.*

Stephen Miles

I watched in horror an undercover report about a lady sentenced to death by stoning without trial. Her husband accused her of adultery; she was driven into the centre of a football stadium filled with men and boys. They cheered and clapped as the poor defenceless lady was mercilessly murdered by stoning. I was left ashamed to be part of the human race; I've never and nor will I ever forget that lady's fate.

Simon Miller is a teacher, playwright and part-time poet. A compulsive traveller, he has spent much of his working life in Africa and Asia. He currently lives in Thailand with his wife and three growing children.

'Offshore': This poem was inspired by the work of Matt Friedman and the teams working against human trafficking in Thailand (www.humantrafficking.org), and reading several online articles about the status of the shrimp fishing industry in Thailand, that 'nets' thousands of vulnerable workers in wage bondage, working in terrible conditions both onshore and for months at sea.

'Dust' is broadly about the refugee experience of dislocation. In the 1990s I was working in southern Africa but whenever I returned to the UK I would repeatedly hear stories from friends about how a flood of 'refugees and illegal immigrants' was now 'ruining' the places in Kent where I grew up. Though most immigration at that time was from Eastern Europe, an awkward juxtaposition developed in my mind between these stories of complaint and what I had seen of a hard rural life in sub-Saharan Africa – not to mention a lack of distinction between the respective plights of migrant workers and refugees. I realised how easy it was to forget how little choice many refugees have in where they end up. 'Dust' is about the inner world that we carry with us that can make dislocation all the more acute for refugees who would rather be 'back home'.

Sohaib Mirza is high in ambition and learning; low in money. Still learning ... recognising barriers in life and injustice.

'Abandoned property' makes reference to Palestinian abandoned property.

Joel Moktar lives in Brixton, south London, and has previously had work published in *Popshot* and *The Cadaverine* magazines.

The original inspiration for 'Lament' is twofold – firstly, the 150th anniversary of the Emancipation Proclamation in January 2013, and secondly Eduardo Galeano's powerful analysis of the political economy of the slave trade in 'Open Veins of Latin America'.

My intentions with this poem were to look beneath the political, economic and legal manifestations of slavery and towards the individual. Indeed, we should not forget it was against millions of individuals that human rights violations took place during the slave trade, and continue to take place in modern forms of slavery today.

The irony, which will become more apparent once you have read the poem, is that I have no idea (thankfully) what 'the lash and tear of leather' feels like. Nonetheless I am certain that imagining and recreating it in our minds can be a huge motivating force in the fight against modern forms of slavery and other similar human rights violations today, as well as allowing us to reflect on what has gone before.

Hubert Moore has had three collections from Enitharmon and three from Shoestring. His eighth collection is due from Shoestring early in 2014. Human rights abuses are a frequent source of poems for him.

'At the approach of dieback' is the result of conversations with survivors of torture, particularly 10 or 12 years after they came here as asylum-seekers when the parents whom they left at home are getting old.

David Lee Morgan has travelled the northern hemisphere as a street musician and performance poet. He has won many poetry slams, including the UK Slam Championship. He is a longstanding member of the Writers Guild and holds a PhD in creative writing from Newcastle University. David lives in London, grew up in the US, was born in Berlin and considers himself a citizen of the planet.

'Dead babies': I read the statistics on world starvation and was stunned.

Duncan Stewart Muir is a Scottish poet, currently living in Beijing, China, where he teaches English and American literature. His poetry has previously been published in magazines and journals in the UK and US, most recently in *PN Review, Blast Furnace* and *Poetry Review.*

'Choeung Ek' was written after travelling to Cambodia, and visiting the main site of genocide, in March 2013. What struck me about Choeung Ek is that we must know what happened there, we must recognise it and see it, and understand why and how it happened. In knowing the terrible things that we, as humans, are capable of, and in trying to understand the reasons behind such atrocities, then we can go further to ensure that such crimes are not carried out again. The poem is the latest in a sequence I have been working on for some time about the Cambodian Genocide. The sequence was initially born from one poem called 'The Chankiri Tree' – named after a tree in The Killing Fields against which children were beaten to death. I first read about this tree on Wikipedia three years ago while studying creative writing in Glasgow. (This poem has since been published in the Scottish literary magazine, Gutter; www. guttermag.co.uk.)

Sai Murray is a poet, writer and graphic artist of Bajan/English/Afrikan heritage. His first volume of poetry *Ad-liberation* is to be published in September 2013. The first part of his debut novel, *Kill myself now* is published by Peepal Tree Press. Sai is the arts and politics editor of *Sable Lit Mag*, artistic director of *Scarf* magazine, and the creative director of Liquorice Fish artist/activist promotions. He was commissioned as poet-in-residence (together with Dorothea Smartt) for C Words; was lead artist on the Re-Membering project, 2010; and was chosen as one of Yorkshire's six most talented literary artists for FWords: Creative Freedom, 2008. Sai has performed, devised and run workshops across the UK and appeared internationally at festivals and venues including: Busboys & Poets (Washington DC), Brave New Voices (San Francisco), Mo Juice Poetry Slam (Barbados). A regular collaborator with musicians, Sai is a member of Manchester-based digital arts collective Virtual Migrants and a resident poet at Numbi. As one of the UK's leading youth poet coaches, Sai has successfully coached winning teams at Leeds Young Authors Voices of a New Generation (2009, 2010, 2012) and at the largest ever UK national slam, Shake the Dust. He is currently a founding poet facilitator (together with Zena Edwards) on Platform's youth arts and campaigning project Shake!, and the creative writing facilitator/mentor with the mental health arts charity Artists in Mind.

'Call Coltan collect' was influenced by the humanitarian crisis in the Congo (DRC) and estimates that over 10 million have died since war began in 1996 – a war driven by the desire to extract raw materials, and in particular the mineral coltan essential for mobile phone technology.

Nie Ren is a Chinese poet born in the 1960s, now based in Guangzhou.

Kate Noakes, Welsh poet, lives mostly in Paris, where she co-founded Paris Lit Up (see parislitup.com). Her most recent collection is *Cape Town* (Eyewear Publishing, 2012).

'The mattress': the homeless are much more visibly present on the streets of Paris than those of London. They are daily in my thoughts, for example, I pass the same ten rough-sleepers, men, women and families with children, at the same points on my commute from Bastille to La Defense.

Benjamin Norris is a poet from Bristol whose work has been featured in a wide range of literary magazines and journals on both sides of the Atlantic. He currently lectures in Indian cultural history at a leading university in Budapest.

'Traffic' was inspired partly by the fact that I live in Bristol – a city which was built on the historical riches of slavery, and which still surprisingly celebrates this shameful history in ways which often seem to overlook the hideous reality of the situation. We have squares named after slavers, festivals which fail to address their origin and many other such examples. However, I also wanted to explore the fact that we often consider slavery to be something of the past, something dealt with and finished. Slavery has not ended, it has simply changed its appearance. I am married to a Romanian woman, who knows people from her town who have been lured into situations of human slavery in the UK, and yet we are hesitant to even use the same words for these situations. My short poem 'Traffic' tries to reflect the present against the past, and whilst the two situations and types of slavery are distinct and separate, we cannot herald the ending of one without acknowledging the continued existence of human trafficking on our shores, our streets, our pleasant market towns.

David Nunn

'The maid I & II': I was drinking coffee outside in a country in the Middle East one evening when a young Asian woman slumped into a nearby seat and placed a holdall on the table. A few minutes later, a couple arrived and the woman jumped up and went to meet them. She took their shopping and young child over to her table, while the man led his wife to a table by a fountain. While they waited for their drinks, the maid changed and fed their child. The drinks arrived and the couple spent a few minutes talking and sipping tea, then the woman snapped her fingers and the maid hurried to place the child in its pushchair next to her. She then returned to her seat, behind the couple's table, out of sight but within earshot.

Soon, the child began to cry and the maid arrived with a bottle. A few minutes later, the child began to cry again. The mother tired of trying to appease the child and signalled to the maid to take the child and leave the couple in peace.

What was striking about this situation was its normality. Almost every family in that country has a live-in maid. Many families in poorer countries send a daughter to a wealthier country to work in order to send money back to support the family. The plight of maids is especially poignant; part of their role is to act as a surrogate mother for their employer's children, while being denied the opportunity to raise their own.

Selina Nwulu is a Yorkshire born, London-based writer and poet. She is a member of the writer's collective Malika's Poetry Kitchen, and her writing, often influenced by her work within environmental and human rights, ranges from observational to political. She has been performing across the UK and beyond for the past two years, most recently in Budapest at an EU environmental human rights conference. Her first chapbook collection is due to be published later this year.

As a campaigner for environmental and social justice, I wrote 'Stop recycling' after being struck time and time again by the cyclical nature of the excuses world leaders employ to justify mass corruption and environmental degradation – whether it be the Nigerian government's collusion with oil corporations such as Shell, and the consequential devastation to communities and ecosystems in the Niger Delta, or the push from the EU for increased dependency on biofuels and the resulting land grabs and food price hikes taking place in many countries in Africa. 'Stop recycling' is a plea for governments worldwide to stop falling back on the same old lies to justify such unsustainable and immoral behaviours and to actually think of new and equality-driven ways that put people and environmental justice at the forefront of global agenda.

Maureen Oliphant worked part-time in adult education at Durham University for many years before starting a home catering business. She cooked all the private dinner parties for Bishop David Jenkins at Auckland Castle and met Desmond Tutu and Mrs Tutu there. She then trained in aromatherapy, reflexology and remedial massage. Now, she just works in the garden. Maureen has won several awards for short stories and poetry and describes herself as a jack of all trades.

'Chained': I am a member of Amnesty International and have been for some years, and I worked at Durham University when Ruth First was a visiting lecturer in the Sociology Department. Ruth First was murdered on her return to South Africa. 'Chained' covers a time of peace and tranquillity followed by the atrocities she and her husband sought to fight against.

David Olsen's third poetry chapbook, *Sailing to Atlantis*, is new from Finishing Line Press, US publisher of *New World Elegies* (2011). In the last year he has placed poems with *Acumen, Envoi, The French Literary Review, SAW Poetry, The Dawntreader, Babel, Sounds of Surprise,* and anthologies from *Cinnamon Press* and *Templar Poetry* (all UK); *Vermont Literary Review, Bloodroot, The Deronda Review, Scintilla,* and *Touch: The Journal of Healing* (US); and *ROPES* (Ireland). He holds an MA in creative writing from San Francisco State University.

Day by day I encounter news stories about the effects of global warming, and the indifference of, or outright denial by, those holding political and economic power. Whatever financial benefits result from continued denial of global warming are not equitably distributed among those who bear the greatest risks of inhabiting a warming planet. Because the vast majority of the world's people will suffer from conditions yielding benefits available only to a tiny minority of powerful people, global warming is a human rights issue.

Richard Ormrod is a biographer, poet and journalist who has taught creative writing for the Open University. He is currently writing the authorised critical biography of the poet Andrew Young (1885–1971).

'Home alone' is a 'protest' poem against the patronising and inadequate treatment of the elderly/demented in the community.

Mandy Pannett is the Poetry Editor for *Sentinel Literary Quarterly*. She also works freelance as a creative writing tutor and poet, leading workshops and taking part in poetry readings. She has won prizes and been placed in international competitions, and has judged several others. Several of her poems have been translated into German and Romanian as part of a translation project. Her novella *The Onion Stone* was published by Pewter Rose Press. Four poetry collections have been published by Oversteps Books, Searle Publishing, and *All the Invisibles*, her latest, by SPM Publications.

'The other side of appearances' is about prisoners of conscience, people who disappear from public view, for years or for life, without the right to a fair trial. I have long been involved with the work of Amnesty International at a local group level, appreciating the good fortune that allows me the freedom of speaking and holding my own opinions without fear of oppression.

An image that inspired me for this poem was the other side of a triptych, the wings as they are called, which are usually far less vibrant and colourful than the side on display, often folded flat against the wall, out of sight and overlooked.

Ryan Paterson is a 20-year-old student of creative writing at the University of Westminster. He was born in South Wales and moved to London to forward his passion for writing, which he began at a young age. Ryan feels writing is a unique way to explore the world.

Growing up as a gay teenager I found the hatred and ignorance against homosexuals, both at home and around the world, very difficult to bear at times. Homophobia and anti-gay opinions were things I could never quite understand, I simply liked boys instead of girls and I couldn't understand why this affected anyone else. I came across a picture online of two students being executed for being gay. The picture horrified me and was one I could never clear from my mind. As a naive boy I couldn't understand why anyone would kill someone for simply loving another human being. I wrote 'Amjad in the sky' to try and articulate the horrors some gay people face around the world today.

Mary Anne Perkins is a retired historian of ideas who lives with her husband on the north-east coast of the UK. Her first collection of poetry, *Shadow-Play*, was published by Indigo Dreams Press in 2009, as the result of winning a collection competition.

'1959' was inspired by news reports in November 2012 on the release of Foreign Office documents by the UK National Archives concerning a massacre in Hola detention camp in Kenya in March 1959. Eleven detainees were beaten to death. Many more were subjected to torture and rape. Colonial officials attempted to cover up the truth that they were responsible, and it was not until October 2012 that three Kenyan men finally won the legal right to pursue a claim against the British government for alleged torture.

The poem throws light on social and cultural attitudes in the 1950s and the climate of opinion which made such injustice possible. There was no procedure for individuals to enforce their rights under the European Convention on Human Rights until the Human Rights Act of 1998. Even then, the procedure did not apply where rights were infringed before the Act came into force.

More recently, the courts have decided that the Act applies to breaches of the Convention by the British Government anywhere in the world; and where the Government behaved unlawfully in a former colony, while acting to maintain its imperial authority, liability for the unlawfulness remained with the British Government instead of passing to the new government when the colony became independent. Thus the Hola massacre can now be recognised as a breach of the Convention (as well as all the other ways in which it was unlawful) for which the British Government remains responsible.

Geralyn Pinto lives in Mangalore, Karnataka, south India. She is an associate professor and head of the PG Department of English at St Agnes College (Autonomous). In 2006, she earned her doctoral degree from the University of Mangalore. Geralyn is a creative writer who has been published and won prizes nationally and internationally. She also works on a part-time and voluntary basis among the ostomy patients of the larger Mangalore area. Geralyn considers herself extremely fortunate for having had a privileged upbringing in terms of the education she received. The curricula were so designed as to give pupils wide 'theoretical' exposure to world culture, history and literature. So she read young about the institution of slavery in the USA; the reservations for First Nation peoples in various parts of the world; apartheid in South Africa, and the American Civil Rights Movement of the mid 20th century. She also read about the White supremacists of the American south and the bloody confrontations between Whites and African Americans in the southern states of the US.

The inspiration for 'Shot through with metal' came from the case of the 1999 police shooting of Amadou Diallo and the subsequent controversial exoneration of those involved. An article in The New York Times *(N.Y./Region, 2 Oct 2012), 'Diallo's mother asks why officer who shot at her son will get gun back' by Wendy Ruderman and J. David Gordon, served as the catalyst for the composition of this poem which highlights historical injustice and the racial unconscious.*

Kathleen M. Quinlan's poetry has been placed in various UK and US literary magazines. A social scientist, her poems explore social issues and have appeared in several social science academic journals. She teaches at the University of Oxford and is a member of Back Room Poets and Second Light Network.

'I might have left' is part of a pamphlet manuscript inspired by my own personal experience with domestic violence. It is one of several poems written specifically to educate the reader about why a woman might stay in such a relationship. When we read stories in the newspapers of women who have lived in abusive relationships, we often wonder why they didn't just leave. Such a question, though, shifts the blame to the victim: 'she should have left'. If she'd left she wouldn't have been beaten, raped, killed. Unfortunately, this kind of thinking – an assumption of the freedom to leave bad circumstances – erodes our empathy and sense of injustice. The perpetrator – whether an anonymous man in a private home or a giant corporation in a community in

a developing country – manages to avoid the full force of our condemnation. I wanted people to understand that there are many ways in which a man might control a woman, making it difficult – or impossible – for her to leave safely.

Usha Raman is a writer, editor and communications professional, currently teaching in the Department of Communication, University of Hyderabad, India. She has published one collection of poetry, *All the spaces in between* (Writers Workshop, Kolkata, India). Other areas of interest include health and science communication and new media studies.

'Kashmir' was inspired by an article in the March 2013 issue of the magazine The Caravan, *entitled 'The Apparatus' by Sanjay Kak, a review essay based on a report on Kashmir, 'Alleged perpetrators'. While I have been reading about life – or what constitutes it – in the Valley, this report was particularly chilling in its detail, and made me wonder about the supposed democracy that I am a part of.*

'Quotidian' is based on a feeling that often strikes me; how does one go on with the ordinary routine of the privileged life when we know how much suffering and injustice there is around us? There is a sense both of hopelessness and powerlessness in the face of the huge inequities and cruelties that seem to surround us. Yet we continue to do the same things, day after day, convincing ourselves at some fundamental level that it's all just the news, something that we can't do anything about.

David Ravelo is an economist, human rights defender and member of the Regional Corporation for the Defence of Human Rights (CREDHOS) in Colombia. A key member of the Barrancabermeja human rights movement, his work involved him denouncing many human rights crimes including forced disappearances, extra-judicial executions and forced displacements. On 5 December 2012 David Ravelo was sentenced to more than 18 years in prison, following 26 months in detention awaiting trial. His conviction for murder followed a process which international human rights organisations and lawyers have criticised for being full of irregularities.

The **Reclaim Shakespeare Company** is a grassroots group campaigning against oil sponsorship of arts and cultural institutions, specifically the Royal Shakespeare Company. In 2012 they performed seven 'stage invasions' before RSC performances in Stratford-upon-Avon and London.

We took inspiration from Shakespearian works for our own mini 'divestment' plays. You can see videos from and information about our protests here: http://bp-or-not-bp.org.

Shane Rhodes has published poetry across Canada and around the world and is the author of four books of poetry which have won a number of national prizes. He is the poetry editor for *Arc*, Canada's national poetry magazine.

'Acts respecting Indians' is about Canada's Indian Act, a statute that allows the Government of Canada to administer registered Indians, their bands and Indian Reserves. The Act sets out who is and isn't an Indian and then describes the special circumstances and limits of their rights. Since its creation in 1876, the Indian Act has been the key legal tool for the Government of Canada's appropriation and management of Aboriginal lands in Canada's ongoing colonisation and settlement. Widely acknowledged as a discriminatory and racist law,

the Indian Act is still in force in Canada and has most recently been challenged because of its specific discriminations against Aboriginal women (who, if they married any other than an Indian man, were no longer considered Indian). 'Acts respecting Indians' uses words directly from the Act to set out the fantastical logic that the Act uses to differentiate who is and isn't a real person under the law, and what makes an 'Indian'.

Orcadian poet **Olive M. Ritch** has been published in a number of literary journals and anthologies including *The Hippocrates Prize 2011* and *The Poetry Cure*. She received a commendation in the National Poetry Competition in 2003 and won the Calder Prize for Poetry at the University of Aberdeen in 2006.

'Mr Hu, the executioner' is based on an article in The Times *(Tuesday 15 November 2011): 'Uneventful, uncomplicated: an executioner's working day'. According to this article 'Mr Hu is a veteran police officer in China whose job involves shooting people convicted of capital crimes, such as murder or rape'. It goes on to say that 'the majority of transplant organs are taken from executed prisoners'.*

Robin Runciman has written many poems addressing human oppression and will continue to do so for as long as he lives.

'Thank you for visiting Deathminster' was inspired by a desire to stand up for humanity in this dark night of insanity. My great friend, Parasuram, a wonderful Hare Krishna monk, came to me to see if I could help him keep his 'Food for All' project alive in the Borough of Camden. Before the Olympics, Camden Council withdrew their funding from this humanitarian project and started fining his vans when they parked up to feed the hungry and homeless on the streets of London. Parasuram has been feeding 1,000 people a day on the streets of Camden for 25 years with simple, tasty, vegetarian food. I was outraged when he told me what had happened.

I was also outraged when some London taxi-driver friends told me how they were being persecuted by fines originating from cameras when they were just doing their jobs. They were being stung with hefty fines for stopping at ATMs for their customers; they were being fined when leaving their cabs for a couple of minutes to go to the toilet, and I heard of instances when Westminster Borough Council fined a taxi driver for taking too long to get a disabled person into his cab.

On driving out of Westminster, one sees a sign saying 'Thank you for visiting Westminster', so I began my poem with 'Thank you for visiting Deathminster'. My dear friend, Andy Boyd, who manages Peter Doherty and the Babyshambles, has come on board to help the 'Food for All' charity stay afloat, raising funds from Babyshambles' forthcoming tour this year. Heartfelt thanks go to Andy and Peter for their spirit of humanity, their generosity and compassion.

Marina Sanchez

'Day of the Dead': the 2007 Law of Historical Memory was passed after a number of highly publicised cases in Spain thrust into the public arena the issue of the victims of the Spanish Civil War (1936–9). The Law requires all bodies in unmarked and mass graves since the Civil War to be exhumed, DNA tested, identified and buried properly. I'd followed the stories closely, but it was reading Giles Tremlett's Ghosts of Spain *and the chapter on the case histories that birthed the poem. I was very struck by the bones being scattered everywhere and people knowing*

about them, but being unable to do anything because of fear. It was such a powerful and clear metaphor that they needed to be laid to rest. So I gave them a voice. The poet Lorca's family has been very vocal in advocating letting things be. But a new generation has been able to bring up the bodies and start the dialogue about the Civil War that has never taken place openly. This is still a very divisive issue in Spain. Due to the blanket political amnesty after Franco's death in 1975, and unlike the South African experience of the Truth and Reconciliation courts, there hasn't been a similar process to channel the repressed feelings that impact on Republicans' families and their descendants. While writing the poem, I was reminded of Hellinger's work on family constellations that suggests that after a war, a nation has to get on with the physical task of rebuilding, leaving the psychic task of healing for later generations, until the collective is ready to deal with the past consciously.

Thanks to this Law, my mother was able to claim a widow's pension because my father was a Republican soldier. He died in exile.

'Under the cross': I went to school in Madrid during Franco's dictatorship and the poem came from my personal experience, which caused me considerable confusion as a child as my father had been a Republican soldier. But I only finished the poem when I watched stills and footage of the Spanish Civil War on YouTube for a song by Ismael Serrano about his grandfather's memories of the conflict. Towards the end of the song, I was struck by photos of the Republican flag, not Franco's, flying today in public places and events. There's a lot of talk in Spain about what will happen when King Juan Carlos dies and there's significant support for a return to the Republic.

The poem's title refers to the Basilica of the Holy Cross of the Valley of the Fallen, the biggest war memorial in the world, built by Franco between 1941 and 1959 by political prisoners, many of whom died because of the conditions in the forced labour camp. There's a lot of controversy about how many political prisoners built the memorial, since Franco's daughter, through her foundation, strives constantly to give his regime a benign gloss. One MP in the Spanish parliament proposed blowing up the monument because it is a reminder of the dictatorship, but the issue is extremely divisive. Every 20 November, on the anniversary of Franco's death, there's a service to a congregation of his supporters wearing Falangist (the Falange is a movement loyal to Franco) uniforms and singing their anthems. When interviewed, the abbot of the Benedictine order that resides there, talks diplomatically about the work being done to promote peace in the mausoleum but everyone knows that it is Franco's tomb and honouring the Republican side is mostly lip service.

Selina Rodrigues has had work published in two Macmillan anthologies focusing on Asian culture and in journals including *Brand, Chroma, Mslexia* and *Magma*. Her poems also feature on The Poetry School website. She has read her work in venues including bookshops and the Poetry Café.

'Organza': people will always move, explore, think and communicate. It's not just through the internet or through talking, but through our senses and imagination. I say I love clothes but what I really mean is that I love colours, textures and shapes. I am hopeless with my hands and value the work of the hairdresser, the plumber and the tailor. Fashion and clothing can say so much, but the environments in which they are produced can be deadly. Article 23, the right to work in just and favourable conditions, is so essential to a healthy and fulfilling life.

Caroline Rooney is an arts activist and academic, and currently directs a Global Uncertainties research programme entitled 'Imagining the Common Ground'.

'Concrete' was written in response to the IDF attack on the 'Mavi Mamara', and its title reflects both the flotilla's intention of bringing concrete to Gaza and the evasions of the media in reporting the attack. 'Al Hurriya Fi Masr' ('Freedom in Egypt') was inspired by a three month visit to Cairo in 2010, including interviews with Egyptian writers and activists, and the subsequent outbreak of the revolution. They are both poems of solidarity.

Bestin Samuel pursues research at the Centre for Comparative Literature, University of Hyderabad, India. His main areas of interest are Dalit studies, ecocriticism, poetry and popular culture. Having completed his MA in English literature from the University of Hyderabad, he worked with Cambridge University Press India before returning to academia. He has presented papers in different national seminars within the country, and is a published poet.

'Superman's Son' deals with the war crimes committed by the Sri Lankan Army towards the end of the 2009 battle with the banned rebel outfit, LTTE. Sri Lanka's comprehensive victory was marred by widespread accusations of the ruthless execution of war prisoners. Balachandra Prabhakaran, the 12-year-old son of the LTTE supremo Veluppilla Prabhakaran (who was killed earlier), was shot dead in cold blood while in custody. Callum Macrae's documentary titled 'No Fire Zone' (screened at the Geneva Human Rights Film Festival at the UN Human Rights Council meeting in March 2013) contains images showing the boy unharmed in custody and having a snack, but other images – taken by the same camera a few hours later – show him lying dead, five bullets having pierced his upper body. The revelation has invited widespread criticism from various countries and organisations, even as the Sri Lankan government denies the allegations.

Richard Scott was born on 30 June 1981 in London. He studied poetry at The Faber Academy and went on to complete an MA in Creative and Life Writing at Goldsmiths. He has since won The Wasafiri New Writing Prize and was selected as a Jerwood/Arvon Poetry Mentee; his mentor was Daljit Nagra. Richard's poetry has been published twice in *Poetry Review*, twice in *Poetry London*, in *Wasafiri Magazine* and he has a poem forthcoming in *Magma*. He has also been commissioned to write a poem for The Southbank Centre, as part of their London Lines, Festival of Literature; his poem 'Dog' was made into a film and exhibited on the Southbank this summer.

I was inspired to write 'Cutting season' after watching The Guardian/Christian Aid *film entitled 'I Will Never Be Cut', by Sara Nason, telling the story of two Kenyan girls, Nancy and Gertrude, rebelling against female circumcision. The poem was inspired by certain phrases spoken by the girls and by their protest.*

Seni Seneviratne is a poet and creative artist of English and Sri Lankan heritage. She has given readings, performances and workshops in the UK, US, Canada, South Africa, Kuwait and Egypt. Her second collection, *The Heart of It*, was published by Peepal Tree Press in April 2012 (www.seniseneviratne.com).

'Naming': in March 2012 a US soldier went on what was described in the press as a killing spree and shot dead 16 civilians, including nine children, in Zangabad village in Kandahar. I was struck by how little information the press gave about the victims in contrast with so much detail about the perpetrator, his life and circumstances. I did some research and at least found out their names. In the poem I wanted to begin to redress the balance.

Jill Sharp works as a tutor with the Open University and runs local writing groups in Swindon, where she is a member of BlueGate Poets. Her poems have appeared in a number of magazines and anthologies, most recently *Fourteen, Poems in the Waiting Room* and online at *Ink, Sweat and Tears*.

'Untouchable' was inspired by a remarkable woman featured in a BBC documentary.

Kerrin P. Sharpe is a poet and teacher of creative writing. She completed the Victoria University Original Composition Programme taught by Bill Manhire in 1976. Her poems have appeared in many journals including *Hue & Cry, JAAM, The Listener, Poetry NZ, Sport, Takahe, Turbine, The London Grip, Snorkel and the Press, Best NZ Poems* (08, 09, 10 and 12), and in *The Best of the Best New Zealand Poems*. In 2008 she was awarded the New Zealand Post Creative Writing Teachers' award from the Institute of Modern Letters. Her debut poetry collection *three days in a wishing well* was published by Victoria University Press in 2012. A selection of her poems will appear in *Oxford Poets 2013* from Carcanet Press later this year.

Vilma's father, a Jewish Professor, was shot in front of the family in World War Two. As she grew older, Vilma's response to this horrific event was to hoard clothing.

Ali Thurm has an MA in French and psychology from the University of St Andrews. She lives in London and is a writer and part-time teacher working with children who speak languages other than English. Ali has published in South Bank Poetry and on the Tate Modern website. She has recently completed 'The Novel Studio' course at City University and is working on her first novel.

'Sewing on jewels' was written in response to the issue of child labour in clothing factories in Asia.

Samuel Tongue was part of the 2010 Glasgow Clydebuilt Verse Apprenticeship scheme, mentored by Liz Lochhead. He currently holds the Callan Gordon Award, part of the Scottish Book Trust's New Scottish Writer Awards for 2013–14. Samuel was recently shortlisted in Magma's Ten Line Poems Competition. He is an affiliate teacher and researcher at the University of Glasgow.

Two media pieces in particular struck me and directly influenced 'Reapers'. One was from *Spiegel Online* called 'Dreams in Infrared: The Woes of an American Drone Operator' by Nicola Abé. This article conducted frank interviews with drone operators from which I lifted the characters of the pilot and the sensor-operator, including the direct and offensive quotation. The effects of the job on the latter are very pronounced and show the psychological wounds of combat at such a geographical and psychological distance in the 'automated battlefield'. The sensor-operator is convinced that a child was killed during one of his operations.

Stephanie Turner is a Keats House Poet, full-time freelance creative artist and artist-in-education. Her work is focused on youth, community cohesion and engagement and she has been facilitating creative workshops in schools, community centres, arts organisations and heritage settings for the past six years.

Mahdi Hashi disappeared last year from Somalia and after six months he appeared in a New York prison. He has been accused of 'terrorism' and he tells his lawyers that he has been subjected to torture, threats and been forced to sign a confession.

His British citizenship was revoked around the same time he was taken by US officials. When he received his British citizenship, his Somali citizenship was rescinded due to Somali law at that time. The UK may have left him stateless.

Mahdi was also one of the 'Muslim community workers' from the Kentish Town Community Organisation that were allegedly systematically harassed and blackmailed by the MI5 in an attempt to recruit them as spies.

Eleanor J. Vale lives in England, and has had poems published in magazines including *Smiths Knoll, Mslexia, The New Writer* and *The Interpreter's House.* Her poetry tends to be founded in life events.

'Women in war': several years ago I heard a young woman talk on Radio 4 about her experience as a woman who was raped in Congo; this is her story as I remember it. News items today show there has been no change in the lot of women in war concerning rape, stigma, poverty wherever there is war.

'Correction': another true story. South Africa – land of beauty, Garden route, Mandela, and where lesbians are 'corrected', persecuted, sometimes to death, and their stories not heard for long enough or loud enough.

Andrew Walton was born in Clydebank, and studied English at the University of Leicester, the city he has lived in since 1995. He has always had a passion for the written word, and has been active politically since the anti-war protests in 2003. Much of his poetry draws inspiration from struggles past and present. So far, his only other published poem is 'Jarrow 2011', on the Youth Fight For Jobs Jarrow re-enactment, in which he took part. However, he is working on developing a body of poetry. Thanks go to Vicky Cowell, to everyone at Word!, Rob Gee and 'Bobba' Bennett of Pinggg,..K, for their generous inspiration and support.

The poem 'Grândola Vila Morena, 2013' refers to the eponymous song by the socialist Portuguese musician, Jose Alfonso. It was one of his few lyrics which was not banned by the fascistic Estado Novo regime, which ruled Portugal for almost 50 years. The breaking point was in 1974, when its broadcast signalled the start of the Carnation Revolution. I have used the repetitive structure of the song as a base for my poem, but updated the sentiment to cover the radicalisation of a new generation of workers internationally against austerity and cuts. We must stand up against neoliberalism and for freedom of speech, democracy and human rights worldwide.

Simon Williams has written poetry for the last 40 years. *A Place Where Odd Animals Stand* (Oversteps Books, 2012) is his fourth published collection, and *He/She* (Itinerant Press, 2013) is his fifth. Simon performs widely, from individual readings to performance poetry events. He has been known to sing.

'Like Water' was inspired by a BBC TV news item which detailed the operation at Queen Elizabeth hospital, Birmingham, to repair the skull of Malala Yousafzai. The 14-year-old Pakistani girl had been shot by Taliban gunmen for her campaigning work to promote the education of girls in her country.

River Wolton grew up in London and lived in Sheffield for 20 years before moving to the Peak District. She was Derbyshire Poet Laureate 2007–9 and works as a writer in the community. Her first collection *Leap* was published by Smith/Doorstop.

The inspiration for 'On rush': the recent periods of flooding in the UK have brought to mind the ongoing and future suffering in other parts of the world with far fewer resources. The statistic that one litre of bottled water takes nine litres of water to produce it (during the manufacturing process etc) stands for the fact that much of what we consume is at the expense of people in developing countries and at the expense of their access to clean water, social justice, health and livelihoods. Without adding extra guilt I wanted to make the connections between consumption in industrial and post-industrial countries, climate change, and the rushing that can overtake us in the urge to acquire more and more 'stuff'.

The inspiration for 'M': for ten years I have volunteered at a group for women who are asylum-seekers and refugees, teaching English and providing social and practical support. We are seeing increasing numbers of women who have been trafficked to the UK. Human trafficking affects an estimated 30 million people worldwide. The details in the poem are based on the story of one woman I have known for the last year, during which time she has been through the asylum process, faced refusal on her first claim for asylum, and then granted 'leave to remain'. She has lost contact with her children who are still in her country of origin, and is trying to trace them. I wanted to highlight the resilience, generosity, adaptability and courage that I witness in people who have survived trauma and forced exile.

Sue Wood has taught at universities in Australia, South Africa and Bradford but now feels at home in Halifax after settling in for 28 years. She has gained commendations in many national poetry competitions, won first prize in the Oxford Literary Festival, is a sometime winner in the Poetry Business Book and Pamphlet Competition, and received the Cinnamon Press Award for Poetry in 2008. This led to the publication of her first poetry collection *Imagine yourself to be water* (2009). Sue ran the part-time creative writing programme at Bradford University, has been writer-in-residence at a Marie Curie Hospice, on the Acute Elderly Wards at Leeds General Infirmary and a writer/facilitator for the Bronte Parsonage Museum. She works with the museums and galleries services as a workshop leader and runs The Creative Doctor as a module on Leeds University's medical degree. A poem from her collection was short-listed for Forward Best Single Poem last year and included in the Forward Anthology 2009.

'Snake guarding a water hole' and 'Elegiac': Sue spent the first years of her academic life teaching in Australia, where she travelled widely. One expedition was across the so-called Dead

*Heart of the desert by train and car. Here she visited Aboriginal mission stations and artists –
an experience that began a life-long interest in Aboriginal art, the plight of a disenfranchised
people whose spiritual and social life was entirely shaped by the land they no longer possessed.
Their 'right' to the land was evident in their images, song and nomadic life punctuated by
'walkabouts'. How such a 'right' could be understood and reinstated by the modern world of
cities and cattle ranches was, and remains, the challenge to Australian society.*

Xidu Heshang is an active Chinese poet now based in Xi'an.

Mantz Yorke has been a teacher and educational researcher. His work has appeared in the
'Best of Manchester Poets' series and elsewhere.

*'Running order BBC Radio 4 News at 8am 1st of August 2012' was conceived when I woke
early on the morning of 1 August 2012 and, as is my habit, turned on Radio 4 for the Today
programme. I was struck by the emphasis given to news items about the Olympics in the
hourly bulletins. Set against developments in Syria and the Sahel, the Olympics seemed to me
to be utterly trivial. Hence this poem: its prosaic nature reflects its origin. It is unfair to pick
on the BBC for poetic criticism, since the shriller press is generally more open to the charge of
trivialisation. The linearity of a radio bulletin, however, does lend itself to the sequencing of
stanzas.*

*'Boreraig': a few years ago I took a circular walk which took in the abandoned village of
Boreraig on the coast of Skye – one of many such abandoned villages on the Isle. I had read
about the Highland Clearances, but walking through the ruins brought home, much more
clearly, the inhumanity of what had been done.*

Kathy Zwick has worked as a social studies teacher in international schools in Brussels,
Tehran and London for over 30 years. Many of her poems deal with the repetitions,
quirks and ironies of history.

*'Terminals: A-Z' was inspired by a teachers' trip to Auschwitz-Birkenau sponsored by the
Holocaust Educational Trust. Imagine 180 normally overly-talkative social studies teachers.
On the return flight we were all silent. I later took a subsequent trip to visit my daughter
working in Tanzania and was struck by the 'World Heritage' status of both Auschwitz and
Stone Town in Zanzibar. I was somewhat disconcerted by their roles as modern 'tourist
attractions'.*

'Mirages of meaning' was recently inspired by reading an article in The Guardian *co-authored
by Glenys Kinnock and Michael E. Capuano, 'A decade on, Sudan threatens to repeat the
tragedy of Darfur' (10 March 2013).*

About the editors

Helle Abelvik-Lawson has a BA in English Language and Literature from the University of Oxford and an MA in Understanding and Securing Human Rights from the Institute of Commonwealth Studies at the University of London. Her research interests include indigenous peoples in the Brazilian Amazon, industry, energy, economics and the environment.

Anthony Hett is a London-based poet from North Wales with an MA in Creative Writing (Plays & Screenplays) from City University London. A member of the Keats House Poets, Anthony has run workshops and performed his Spoken Word Poetry throughout England & Wales. He is currently working on a one-man play and his first full collection of poetry.

Laila Sumpton is a member of the Keats House Poets and also a graduate of the Institute of Commonwealth Studies' MA in Understanding and Securing Human Rights. She works both in the NGO sector for Plan UK and as a poet, running poetry workshops and events and writing human rights poetry.

Index of first lines

In December '66, when the
    harmattan blew hot, 164
In the interests of the Indians, 32
I shouldn't even, 181
It came to pass, 52
It is not my decision, 162
It looked as if about to become very
    nasty, 196
I try to make myself at home after
    seeing your heartfelt smile, 8
It's interesting, this electrode they've,
    163
It's sixty-seven years since her
    parents, 27
It was raining outside, 61
I've never had to silence thought,
    203
I want to hear their names. The
    names, 4
Joseph – he wears that coat like an
    oily skin, 59
June 10th, 1989. At 7 p.m., on a
    street in Haikou, 193
Land is everywhere about us, 37
lend me a single syllable, 74
Like a raindrop suspended from a
    twig, 118
Like everyone else, I turned this into
    a verb, 62
Loveless as sandpaper, the boatman's
    cry, 120
Mamadou was as light as chaff, 84
Méiyǔ, 173
Money you entered my soul early,
    earlier than I could speak, 174
my eyes were not green for you, 2
My mother stayed between borders,
    68
Named after Joseph, 49
Nights, so many nights, 112

No more, 106
one night, 144
On the morning they kill Troy Davis,
    105
On the weekend, I seek asylum in
    the arms of some Kylie, 56
Orphans. Maimed ones. Not the
    pretty able-bodied ones, 90
Our footsteps follow wakes.
    Consider, 128
Perhaps they were wrong, 25
pushed hard, and whipped through
    kindly straits, 128
Rising before the sun, 177
Rising eleven, we've got the hang of
    things, 19
Sat in the House of Commons, a
    minister now debates with no
    members, 187
She does her prayers as usual, 136
she had never enough dresses, 54
She opens shop along its muddy
    shore, 149
She shines like Lakshmi through the
    fields, 183
She went looking for her daughter.
    How many, 63
So I'll recycle, 46
Some bleached, others jutting, 73
Someone had come with her, 66
stuck in my skull: a switch & needle,
    163
Terrorism is a way of life, 7
Terror! Terror! Where are the
    terrorists?, 64
Thank you for visiting Deathminster,
    188
that Cain slew Abel, 52
that first time, when, 140
that many have tried to tame, 43

Index of titles

CPSIA information can be obtained
at www.ICGtesting.com
Printed in the USA
FSHW020913090321
79299FS

9 780957 521032